Upper Columbia Basin Network
Integrated Water Quality Annual Report 2010

John Day Fossil Beds National Monument (JODA)

Natural Resource Technical Report NPS/UCBN/NRTR—2012/579

Eric Starkey

Aquatic Biologist
Upper Columbia Basin Network Inventory and Monitoring Program
105 E. 2nd St.
Suite #7
Moscow, ID 83843

June 2012

U.S. Department of the Interior
National Park Service
Natural Resource Stewardship and Science
Fort Collins, Colorado

The National Park Service, Natural Resource Stewardship and Science office in Fort Collins, Colorado publishes a range of reports that address natural resource topics of interest and applicability to a broad audience in the National Park Service and others in natural resource management, including scientists, conservation and environmental constituencies, and the public.

The Natural Resource Technical Report Series is used to disseminate results of scientific studies in the physical, biological, and social sciences for both the advancement of science and the achievement of the National Park Service mission. The series provides contributors with a forum for displaying comprehensive data that are often deleted from journals because of page limitations.

All manuscripts in the series receive the appropriate level of peer review to ensure that the information is scientifically credible, technically accurate, appropriately written for the intended audience, and designed and published in a professional manner.

Data in this report were collected and analyzed using methods based on established, peer-reviewed protocols and were analyzed and interpreted within the guidelines of the protocols.

Views, statements, findings, conclusions, recommendations, and data in this report do not necessarily reflect views and policies of the National Park Service, U.S. Department of the Interior. Mention of trade names or commercial products does not constitute endorsement or recommendation for use by the U.S. Government.

This report is available from the Upper Columbia Basin Network (http://www.nature.nps.gov/im/units/ucbn/) and the Natural Resource Publications Management website (http://www.nature.nps.gov/publications/nrpm/).

Please cite this publication as:

Starkey, E. N. 2012. Upper Columbia Basin Network integrated water quality annual report 2010: John Day Fossil Beds National Monument (JODA). Natural Resource Technical Report NPS/UCBN/NRTR—2012/579. National Park Service, Fort Collins, Colorado.

NPS 177/114294, June 2012

Contents

Contents (continued)

Figures

Figures (continued)

Tables

Appendices

Executive Summary

The mission of the National Park Service is "to conserve unimpaired the natural and cultural resources and values of the national park system for the enjoyment of this and future generations" (NPS 1999). To uphold this goal, the Director of the NPS approved the Natural Resource Challenge to encourage national parks to focus on the preservation of the nation's natural heritage through science, natural resource inventories, and expanded resource monitoring (NPS 1999). Through the Challenge, 270 parks in the national park system were organized into 32 inventory and monitoring networks. The Upper Columbia Basin Network (UCBN) is comprised of 8 national park sites located in Idaho, Montana, Oregon, and Washington.

The UCBN has identified 14 priority park vital signs, indicators of ecosystem health, which represent a broad suite of ecological phenomena operating across multiple temporal and spatial scales. The intent of the network is to monitor a balanced and integrated "package" of vital signs that meets the needs of current park management, but will also be able to accommodate unanticipated environmental conditions in the future. Water quality is a particularly high priority vital sign for six of the nine UCBN parks. The UCBN contains more than 34 rivers, streams, ponds, and reservoirs. Unlike many National Parks that are large and often encompass entire watersheds, most UCBN parks and water bodies are small and embedded in large watersheds with diverse land use.

This annual report details the status of key indicators of water quality obtained from monitoring in John Day Fossil Beds National Monument (JODA). Monitoring occurred in two units of JODA, Painted Hills and Sheep Rock. Bridge Creek flows through the Painted Hills unit and the John Day River flows through the Sheep Rock unit. Data from the 2010 field sampling effort was collected following methods detailed in the UCBN integrated water quality monitoring protocol (Starkey et al. 2008). The UCBN Integrated Water Quality Monitoring Protocol was formally peer-reviewed and approved for implementation in August 2009. This protocol can be found on the UCBN website at:
http://science.nature.nps.gov/im/units/ucbn/reports/index.cfm#IWQ_Mon. Benthic macroinvertebrates were collected by the United States Forest Service- PACFISH/INFISH Biological Opinion (PIBO) according to their peer reviewed protocol during the UCBN's monitoring of stream channel characteristics and riparian condition in 2010. The UCBN's peer reviewed stream channel characteristics and riparian condition protocols can also be found on the UCBN's website listed above.

Water chemistry and macroinvertebrate results indicate that the Bridge Creek and the John Day River are in fair condition, with the primary concern being elevated water temperatures The status of water quality for Bridge Creek and the John Day River relative to state regulatory thresholds is given in the summary tables on the following page. UCBN water quality monitoring is conducted on a 3 year rotating panel. As a result, conditions in both Bridge Creek and the John Day River will be re-evaluated in 2013.

Note that several of the appendices in this report are primarily intended for UCBN internal reference. In addition, some appendices serve as hard copies of quality assurance/quality control procedures performed during data processing.

Bridge Creek Water Chemistry Summary 2010

Measure	Current Condition (June-November, 2010)	State DEQ Thresholds	% Exceedance[a]
Temperature (*MDMT, **MDAT)	* MDMT= 23.57 °C ** MDAT= 19.78 °C	7 day average < 18 °C (salmon/trout rearing/migration)	12.5 %
Total dissolved solids /TDS (mean)	200 mg/L	TDS < 500 mg/L	0 %
Dissolved oxygen (mean daily min)	8.70 mg/L	> 6.5 mg/L instantaneous (cool water, non-spawning)	0 %
pH (mean daily max)	8.54 pH Units	9.0 pH Units	< 1 %
pH (mean daily min)	8.22 pH Units	6.5 pH Units	0 %
Turbidity (mean daily max)	31.48 NTU	< 10% cumulative increase in natural stream turbidities may be allowed, as measured relative to a control point immediately upstream of the turbidity causing activity	Insufficient data
E. coli	220 MPN/100 ml	< 406 E. coli/100 ml	0 %

John Day River Water Chemistry Summary 2010

Measure	Current Condition (June-November, 2010)	State DEQ Thresholds	% Exceedance[a]
Temperature (*MDMT, **MDAT)	* MDMT= 26.44 °C ** MDAT= 23.0 °C	7 day average < 18 °C (salmon/trout rearing/migration)	50 %
Total dissolved solids /TDS (mean)	210 mg/L	TDS < 500 mg/L	0 %
Dissolved oxygen (mean daily min)	7.77 mg/L	> 6.5 mg/L instantaneous (cool water, non-spawning)	< 1 %
pH (mean daily max)	8.58 pH Units	9.0 pH Units	0 %
pH (mean daily min)	8.14 pH Units	6.5 pH Units	0 %
Turbidity (mean daily max)	73.16 NTU	< 10% cumulative increase in natural stream turbidities may be allowed, as measured relative to a control point immediately upstream of the turbidity causing activity	Insufficient data
E. coli	9 MPN/100 ml	< 406 E. coli/100 ml	0 %

*MDMT – Maximum Daily Maximum Temperature, **MDAT – Maximum Daily Average Temperature, [a] Proportion of samples above water quality standard.

0-5% exceedance	
5-25% exceedance	
>25% exceedance	

Acknowledgments

Funding for this project was provided through the National Park Service Natural Resource Challenge and the Servicewide Inventory and Monitoring Program.

Introduction and Background

Water resources have been identified as a high priority vital sign for the Upper Columbia Basin Network (UCBN). These resources are used by many riparian, migratory, and terrestrial organisms in the Network, and have intrinsic value as places of natural beauty and recreation (Garrett et al. 2007). Reflecting this priority, the Water Resources Division (WRD) of the NPS provides a separate source of funding each fiscal year to the UCBN to accomplish water quality monitoring. In June 2010 the UCBN began its first year of integrated water quality monitoring in the Bridge Creek and the John Day River at John Day Fossil Beds National Monument (JODA).

Water resources in the semi-arid West have been strongly affected by human activity, and all UCBN streams and rivers are listed by states as impaired for one or more parameters. Most UCBN water bodies and many aquatic resources such as migratory fish are strongly influenced by activities in the larger watersheds outside park boundaries. Understanding the current status of freshwater ecosystems will help guide management and restoration efforts, and provide insight into ecosystem change in a landscape with a shifting climate and dynamic human influences.

During the process of prioritizing vital signs to monitor in UCBN parks in 2005, water quality was identified as a high priority vital sign (Garrett et al. 2007). When asked what aspects of water quality were important to monitor, resource managers identified the sampling of macroinvertebrate assemblages within UCBN water bodies as the top water quality monitoring priority. Secondary priorities included baseline sampling of water chemistry parameters, characterization of channel morphology, and information on water quantity. Channel morphology and riparian vegetation will be addressed in separate monitoring protocols which are under development.

The objectives of the UCBN Integrated Water Quality Monitoring Protocol are documenting the aquatic macroinvertebrate assemblage composition and baseline water chemistry parameters. Aquatic macroinvertebrate assemblages have strong effects on freshwater ecosystem processes and represent an important trophic linkage between primary producers and fishes. Measures of macroinvertebrate assemblage composition and structure have been frequently used as water quality indicators because these assemblages integrate the effects of point and non-point source pollutants over spatial-temporal scales and can be used to answer many management questions. Also, macroinvertebrates are more cost-effective to sample than other biota or many water chemistry parameters.

Water chemistry and temperature have strong effects on aquatic biota. Consequently, direct and indirect human alteration of stream water quality is associated with altered biotic communities and ecosystem processes. Because of the direct relationship between water chemistry and biota, water chemistry is typically a central component of any water quality monitoring program. More recently, monitoring of stream water temperatures has increased in the Pacific Northwest, because of concerns over cold-water fish habitat (primarily salmonid fishes), the recognized influence of land- and water-use on stream temperature regime, and the need for baseline temperature information to monitor the effects of climate change. National Park Service (NPS) Water Resource Division (WRD) has identified a suite of four "core water quality parameters": temperature, specific conductance, pH, and dissolved oxygen, which are critical to understanding baseline conditions in aquatic habitats. The UCBN added turbidity as a parameter to measure because turbidity is listed as a source of impairment in several UCBN park streams.

Well articulated desired future condition statements have not yet been developed for water quality in UCBN parks. However, the mission statements for the NPS as a whole and for the individual parks clearly state the intent "to conserve unimpaired the natural and cultural resources and values of the national park system for the enjoyment of this and future generations" (NPS 1999). Water quality is a particularly important resource with nationally recognized merit. It is assumed that desired future conditions for all UCBN parks will include clean streams, rivers, and lakes free of human health concerns that provide visitors with recreational and scenic experiences. Monitoring macroinvertebrate assemblage composition and structure, and core water quality parameters will directly measure the water characteristics most important to park mission, visitor experience, and desired future conditions.

Objectives

The overarching programmatic goal of the UCBN integrated water quality monitoring program is to obtain information that will aid in informed management decisions pertaining to improved water quality within UCBN parks. Park managers have committed to improving the water quality of impaired waters by adopting the NPS Government Performance Results Act (GPRA) goal (Ia4) that streams and rivers managed by NPS will meet State and Federal water quality standards (NPS 2000). Most UCBN waters do not meet standards and are listed on EPA 303(d) lists.

Given the lack of available data on water quality in UCBN parks, the following fundamental questions drive much of the UCBN's inquiry into water quality:

- Are the core water quality parameters of streams in the UCBN with established Total Maximum Daily Loads (TMDLs) selected for sampling improving over time?
- What is the status and long-term trend of core water quality parameters (temperature, pH, conductivity, dissolved oxygen, and turbidity) in UCBN streams selected for sampling?
- What is the status and long term trend in aquatic macroinvertebrate abundance and assemblage composition in selected UCBN streams?
- Do aquatic macroinvertebrate assemblages sampled within UCBN streams indicate polluted or otherwise impaired water quality?
- Do aquatic macroinvertebrate assemblages sampled within UCBN streams indicate "pristine" or "reference" conditions according to regional criteria established by Environmental Protection Agency (EPA) and the states of Idaho, Oregon, Montana, and Washington?

In light of these questions and the broader goals outlined above, water quality monitoring in the UCBN addresses the following specific measurable monitoring objectives:

- Determine status and long term trend in key water quality parameters for selected streams within UCBN park units.
- Determine status and trend in aquatic macroinvertebrate abundance, assemblage composition, and functional feeding group composition in wadeable streams within the UCBN.

Study Area

John Day River- John Day Fossil Beds National Monument (JODA), Sheep Rock Unit

The Sheep Rock unit of JODA is in the Upper John Day Watershed, Hydrologic Unit 17070201 (United States Geologic Survey [USGS]), in Grant County, Oregon (Figures 1 and 2, Appendix B). The drainage area for the John Day River above the park is approximately 4,351 square km (1,680 square miles) and consists of several land cover types (NPS 1997). According to Bell and Hinson 2010, Sheep Rock's watersheds are dominated by the following land cover types: big sagebrush-bluebunch wheatgrass (*Aretimisia tridentate, Pseudoroegneria spicata*) (36.59%), Wyoming big sagebrush (*Aretimisia tridentata* spp. *wyomingensis*) (13.63%), and has less than 3% of the watersheds in agriculture or developed lands. In addition, over 25% of the Sheep Rock watersheds are tree dominated vegetation, primarily ponderosa pine (*Pinus ponderosa*) and Douglas fir (*Pseudotsuga menziesii*)[Bell and Hinson 2010].

Threats to water resources in JODA have been listed as: irrigation withdrawals, confined animal feeding upstream and untreated sewage effluent from upstream (Garrett et al. 2007). In addition, the John Day River is listed as impaired in the following areas based on 303(d) criteria: temperature, dissolved oxygen and bacteria (OR DEQ 2010).

Designated beneficial uses for the John Day River and all its tributaries include: public and private domestic water supply, industrial water supply, irrigation, livestock watering, fish and aquatic life, wildlife and hunting, fishing, boating, water contact recreation, and aesthetic quality (OR DEQ 2010). Designated fish use is for salmon and trout rearing and migration (note: includes all salmon species, steelhead, rainbow and cutthroat trout. The designated salmon and steelhead spawning use is from January 1 – May 15(OR DEQ 2010).

The Hydrolab was deployed approximately 1.6 km downstream of the Cant ranch house and approximately 200 m downstream of the first parking area north of the Cant ranch (Figure 3 and Appendix A). This location was chosen due to logistical considerations, adequate water depth, and to avoid placement of equipment near river access points. The macroinvertebrate sample reaches along the John Day River coincide with the stream channel characteristics and riparian condition monitoring reaches (see Appendix C for GPS waypoint).

Figure 1. John Day River looking upstream towards picture gorge.

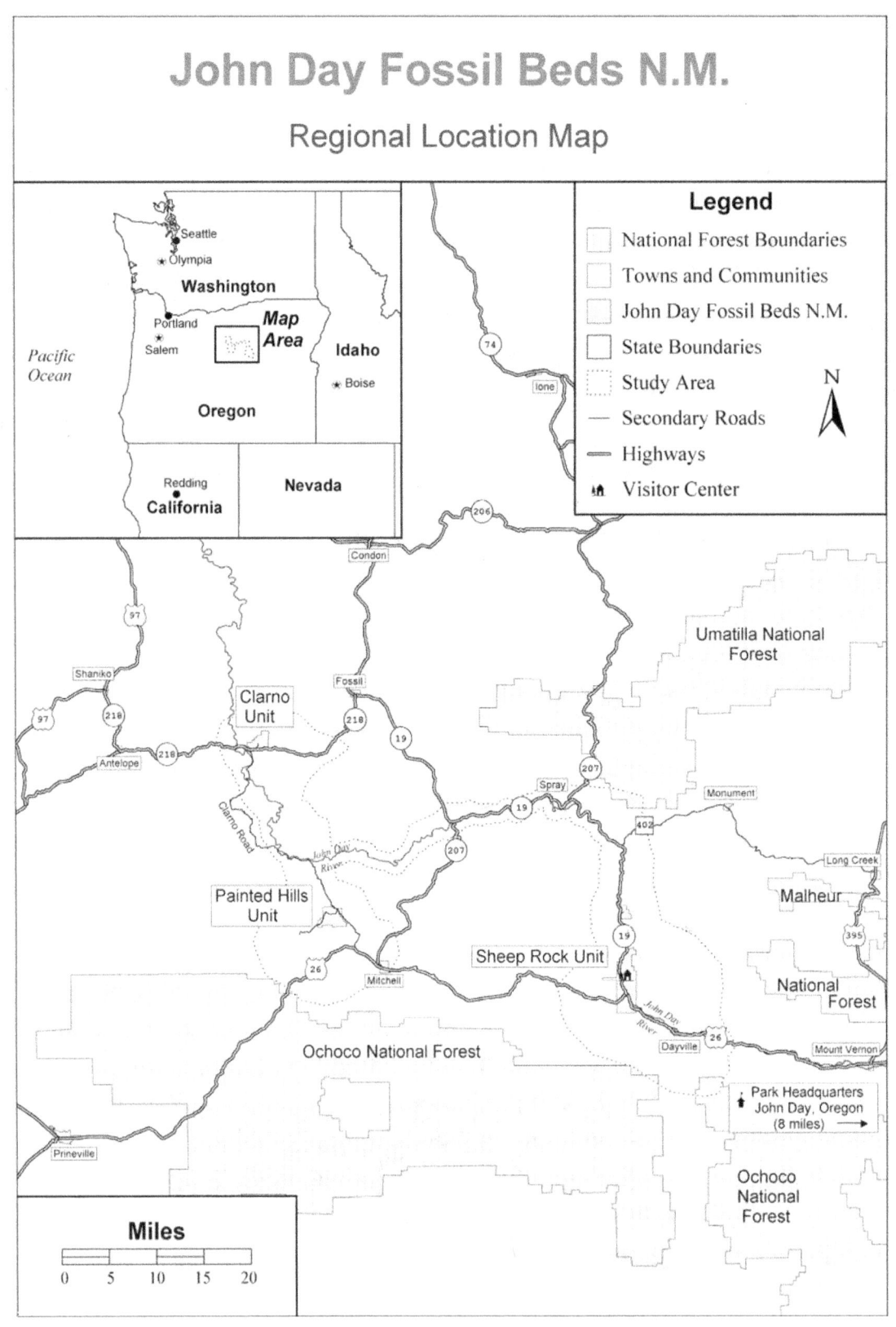

Figure 2. John Day Fossil Beds National Monument regional map (NPS 1997).

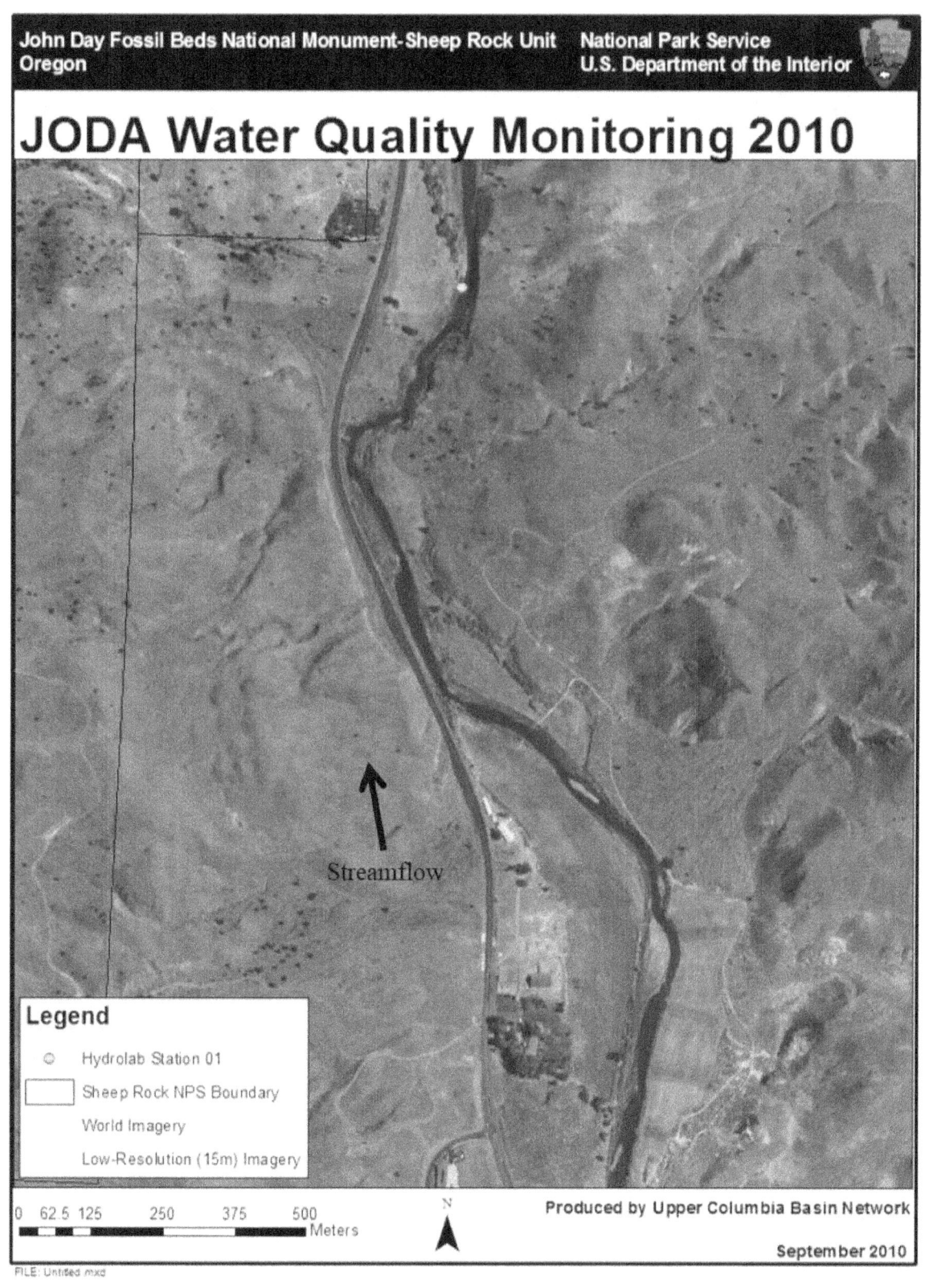

Figure 3. Water quality monitoring location in the John Day River 2010.

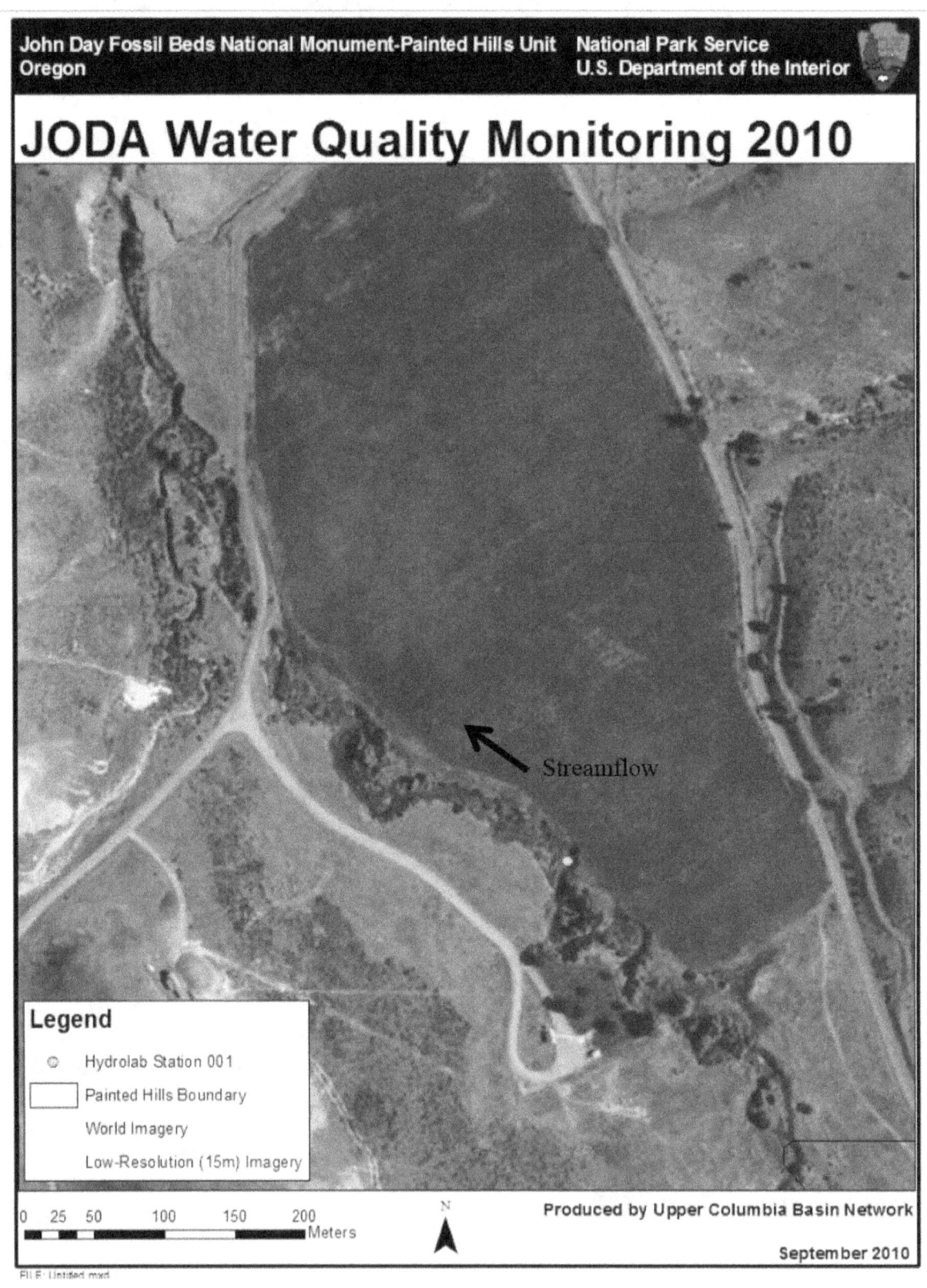

Figure 4. Water quality monitoring location in Bridge Creek 2010.

Bridge Creek- John Day Fossil Beds National Monument (JODA), Painted Hills Unit

The Painted Hills unit of JODA is in the Lower John Day Watershed, Hydrologic Unit 17070204 (United States Geologic Survey [USGS]), in Wheeler County, Oregon (Figures 2 and 5, Appendix B). The drainage area for Bridge Creek above the USGS gage (#14046778) is approximately 692 square km (267 square miles) and consists of several land cover types (NPS 1997). According to Bell and Hinson 2010, the Painted Hills watersheds are dominated by the following land cover types: big sagebrush-bluebunch wheatgrass (40.34%), Wyoming big sagebrush (33.06%), and less than 2% of the watersheds in agriculture or developed lands.

Threats to water resources in JODA have been listed as: irrigation withdrawals, confined animal feeding upstream and untreated sewage effluent from upstream (Garrett et al. 2007). In addition, Bridge Creek is listed as impaired for temperature (2004/2006 OR DEQ 303(d) list).

Designated beneficial uses for the Bridge Creek include: public and private domestic water supply, industrial water supply, irrigation, livestock watering, fish and aquatic life, wildlife and hunting, fishing, boating, water contact recreation, and aesthetic quality (OR DEQ 2010). Designated fish use is for salmon and trout rearing and migration (note: includes all salmon species, steelhead, rainbow and cutthroat trout. The designated salmon and steelhead spawning use is from January 1 – May 15(OR DEQ 2010).

The Hydrolab was deployed approximately 75 m downstream of the picnic area /visitor information kiosk (Figure4 and Appendix A). This location was chosen due to logistical considerations, adequate water depth, and to avoid placement of equipment near creek access points

Figure 5. Bridge Creek looking upstream towards the picnic area.

Methods

Water Chemistry

Continuous water quality monitors (HACH, MS5 Hydrolabs) were deployed from June 25th to November 4th in the John Day River, and from June 26th to November 3rd in Bridge Creek at index sites to estimate the status, variability, and long-term trends in core parameters. The core parameters measured were water temperature, dissolved oxygen, pH, specific conductance, and turbidity. These core parameters were measured hourly and the instrument serviced monthly throughout the deployment period. Each monitor was deployed in a location that was representative of conditions in the park, logistically feasible to access, and relatively secure from vandalism and high flows. A cross-section survey was conducted to aid in the determination of Hydrolab site selection. For more information on the UCBN water chemistry sampling design see Starkey et al. (2008). It should be noted that on Bridge Creek, a gap in monitoring occurred from August 5th to August 25th when Hydrolab #054 was sent to the Hach Company for repair. This instrument was re-installed on August 25th.

Quality Assurance/Quality Control (QA/QC):

Quality assurance and quality control for multiprobe data collection are covered in detail in SOP #12 (Starkey et al. 2008). Basic procedures adhere to the guidelines established in Part B lite (Irwin 2008); the National Coastal Assessment Quality Assurance Project Plan 2001-2004 (U.S. EPA 2001); the Laboratory Methods Manual-Estuaries, Volume 1: Biological and Physical Analyses (U.S. EPA 1995); and Rapid Bioassessment Protocols for Use in Streams and Wadeable Rivers (Barbour et al. 1999).

General quality assurance and quality control methods for UCBN water quality multiprobe calibration and data downloads include the following:

- Representative multiprobe sample locations are determined by using a cross-section and stream segment survey. Each site is re-assessed for representativeness at the start and end each sample year.

- The UCBN follows pre-established maximum acceptable differences for field instrument calibration and QC checks. If the multiprobe readings are outside of the maximum acceptable differences, the multiprobe is removed for non-routine maintenance.

- When calibrating the multiprobe, values of known standard solutions are measured pre and post calibration, to help determine if the instrument's measurements have "drifted." In addition, repeated measures of these solutions are used to determine the repeatability of multiprobe measures.

- All multiprobe data is visually checked for outliers and QC issues immediately following the download of data. QC issues indicated by the data may include: wiper parking, defective sensors, power supply problems, and other anomalies affecting data quality.

- Quantitative and qualitative terms that describe how accurate data need to be in order to meet project objectives are discussed in detail in SOP #12 Starkey et al. 2008 and

Appendix D in this report. NPS WRD lists the following data quality objectives as necessary for water chemistry data: target population, representativeness, completeness, data comparability, measurement sensitivity and detection limits, measurement precision as repeatability, and measurement systematic error/bias.

More detailed QA/QC for water quality multiprobes is contained in SOP #6 and 12, Starkey et al. 2008.

Discharge

Gaging stations on the John Day River are located far enough from the park to make them marginally useful for determination of discharge within the park. The closest active gages on the John Day River are USGS #14038530 near John Day, OR (≈60 km upstream of water quality monitoring station) and USGS #14046500 at Service Creek, OR (≈70 km downstream). The closest historic gaging station on the John Day River is USGS #14040500 at Picture Gorge, near Dayville, OR (≈5 km upstream of water quality monitoring station). This gage was active from 1926 to 1991.

The only gage on Bridge Creek is USGS # 14046778 Bridge Creek above Coyote Canyon near Mitchell, OR (≈12 km downstream of water quality monitoring station). This gage is useful for the determination of general flow conditions within the Painted Hills Unit.

Macroinvertebrates

On the John Day River, macroinvertebrates were collected at 6 sample reaches by the United States Forest Service- PACFISH/INFISH Biological Opinion (PIBO) Effectiveness Monitoring Program during the assessment of stream channel characteristics. This assessment was completed as part of the UCBNs stream channel characteristics monitoring protocol. Macroinvertebrates were collected from 8 fast water habitats (riffles, runs) in each sample reach. These 8 samples were combined for a single composite sample per reach. For more information on the PIBO macroinvertebrate sampling design see Heitke et al. (2008).

Bridge Creek is part of the Intensively Monitored Watershed project implemented by NOAA Fisheries, Northwest Fisheries Science Center. Due to the extensive monitoring of Bridge Creek by NOAA the UCBN did not collect benthic macroinvertebrates in 2010. The methods used by NOAA to collect macroinvertebrates are based on those used by PIBO and are outlined in Weber (2009). More information on the intensively monitored restoration of Bridge Creek can be found in Pollock (2007), ISEMP (2009), and Hall et al. (2010).

Coliform

At the request of the park, coliform samples were collected to determine baseline counts for total coliform, fecal coliform and *E. coli*. Note that coliform sampling is not routinely performed as part of the Integrated Water Quality Protocol. One sample was taken from the John Day River in Picture Gorge (August 25th, 2010) and another sample drawn from Bridge Creek near the picnic area (August 26th, 2010). Samples were chilled and transported to Table Rock Analytical Laboratory in Pendleton, OR for analysis.

Results

John Day River- Sheep Rock Unit

Water Chemistry:

Cross Section Survey:
A cross section survey was conducted at the proposed multiprobe deployment location to evaluate if the site was reasonably representative of stream conditions throughout the park. As suggested by the water resource division the UCBN judges overall representativeness primarily on the basis of specific conductance (Starkey et al. 2008).

The 2010 deployment location provided adequate water depth throughout the field season, was easily accessible, and was away from heavily trafficked river access points. There are limited other deployment locations along the river due to the proximity of the highway, frequent visitor use and lack of pools.

A one way analysis of variance (ANOVA) test was conducted to evaluate representativeness (R v2.12.0). Results of the ANOVA showed that there was a significant difference for specific conductance among the transects and the deployment location in August $F_{(4,42)}=17.06$, p $=2.205e-08$ and no significant difference in November $F_{(4,38)}= 0.7694$, p $= 0.5519$ (Figures 6 and 7).

To determine where the difference in representativeness occurred, a post hoc Tukey's test was conducted (R v2.12.0). Relative to specific conductance, results of the Tukey's test for the cross section conducted in August indicates that the deployment location was significantly different from transects 2, 3, and 4.

In summary, the deployment location was less representative in August than in November; however, this pool and segment of stream likely remains one of the best deployment locations within the park.

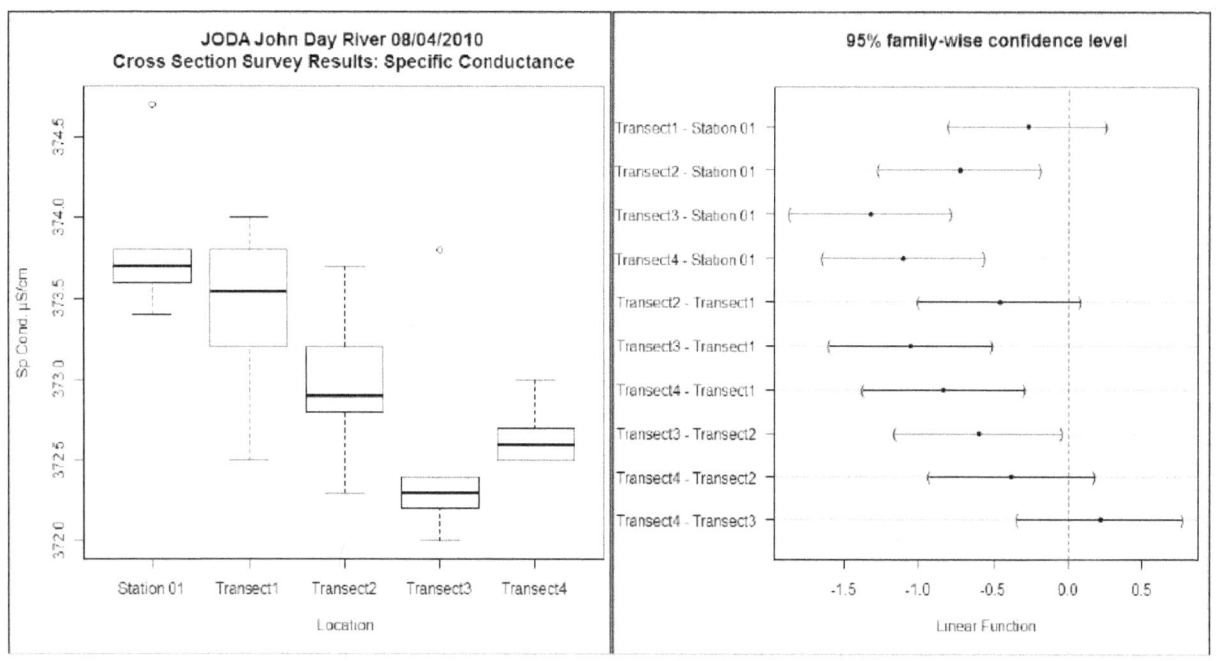

Figure 6. August 2010 cross section survey of the John Day River, box plot of specific conductance and plot of 95% family-wise confidence level.Note that "Station 01" is the location of multiprobe deployment and the transects progress upstream (1-4).

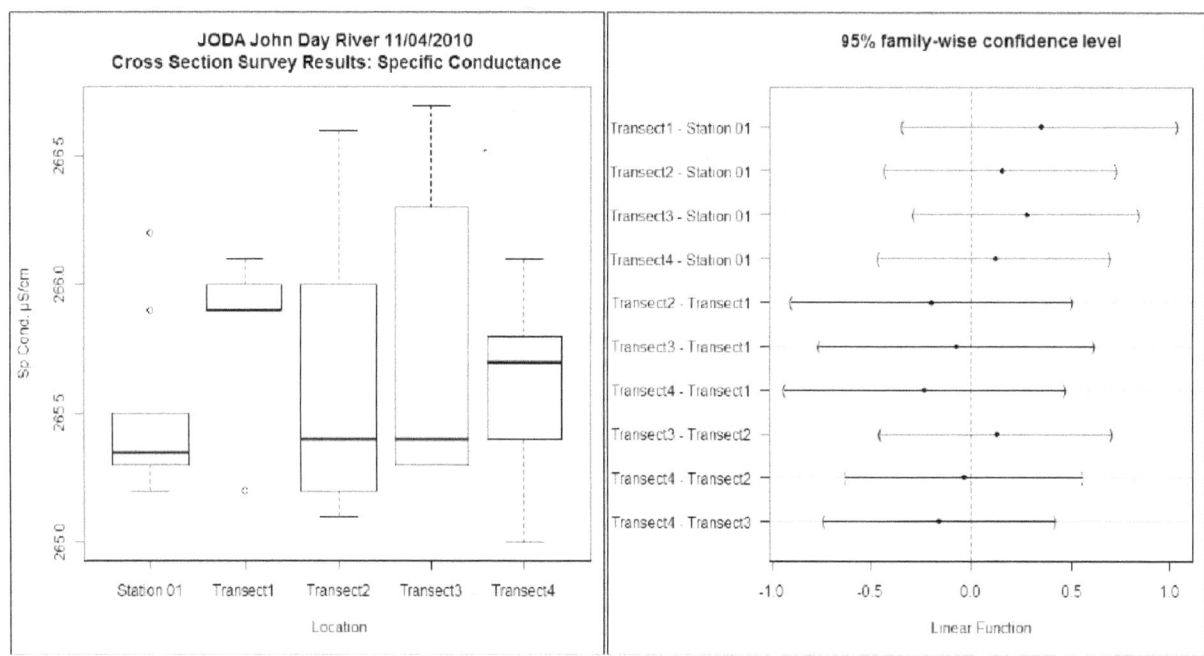

Figure 7. November 2010 cross section survey of the John Day River, box plot of specific conductance and plot of 95% family-wise confidence level.Note that "Station 01" is the location of multiprobe deployment and the transects progress upstream (1-4).

Status:

Condition of core water quality parameters along with the corresponding state Department of Environmental Quality (DEQ) regulatory threshold are given in Table 1. The primary concern is elevated water temperatures and their effect on native salmonids. In most cases, the lowest dissolved oxygen content coincided with elevated water temperatures. Each parameter is discussed in further detail below.

Table 1. Vital sign summary table for water chemistry in the John Day River June-November, 2010

John Day River Water Chemistry Summary 2010

Measure	Current Condition (June-November, 2010)	State DEQ Thresholds	% Exceedance[a]
Temperature (*MDMT, **MDAT)	* MDMT= 26.44 °C ** MDAT= 23.0 °C	7 day average < 18 °C (salmon/trout rearing/migration)	50 %
Total dissolved solids /TDS (mean)	210 mg/L	TDS < 500 mg/L	0 %
Dissolved oxygen (mean daily min)	7.77 mg/L	> 6.5 mg/L instantaneous (cool water, non-spawning)	< 1 %
pH (mean daily max)	8.58 pH Units	9.0 pH Units	0 %
pH (mean daily min)	8.14 pH Units	6.5 pH Units	0 %
Turbidity (mean daily max)	73.16 NTU	< 10% cumulative increase in natural stream turbidities may be allowed, as measured relative to a control point immediately upstream of the turbidity causing activity	Insufficient data
E. coli	9 MPN/100 ml	< 406 E. coli/100 ml	0 %

*MDMT – Maximum Daily Maximum Temperature **MDAT – Maximum Daily Average Temperature

0-5% exceedance	
5-25% exceedance	
>25% exceedance	

- *Temperature:*
  The 7 day average temperature exceeded 18.0 °C in 50% of observations and the maximum daily maximum temperature (MDMT) was 26.4 °C. Our data reinforces basin-wide temperature concerns as discussed in the John Day River Basin Total Maximum Daily Load (TMDL) and Water Quality Management Plan (OR DEQ 2010). Figure 8 shows the daily maximum and mean daily temperatures in the John Day River from June-November 2010. Figure 9 shows the data rating/grade for each deployment period (monthly interval). These standard USGS ratings are based on the degree of sensor fouling and drift encountered during each deployment period (Wagner et al. 2006; Starkey et al. 2008).

  Water temperatures are of particular interest in the John Day River, given that its designated fish use is for salmon and trout rearing and migration (note: includes all salmon species, steelhead, rainbow and cutthroat trout). Elevated water temperatures can be caused by poor stream shading and dewatering. It is important to note that elevated water temperatures have the capacity to reduce the total concentration of dissolved oxygen (i.e., there is an inverse relationship between water temperature and dissolved oxygen; Figure 13), thereby impacting aquatic biota. Implications of elevated water temperatures may include decreased salmonid recruitment, decreased salmonid health, and potential shifts in fish and benthic macroinvertebrate communities (Vannote and Sweeney 1980; McCullough 1999).

Maintaining water temperatures suitable for naturally occurring species in the John Day River will depend on riparian condition and reduced dewatering basin-wide. For this reason cooperation with other agencies, stakeholders, and adjacent landowners will be critical for improving water temperature.

- *Specific Conductance:*
  Specific conductance ranged from 224.0 to 406.0 µS/cm, with an average specific conductance of 336.4 µS/cm. There is no regulatory threshold for specific conductance but rather a threshold for total dissolved solids (see section below). The sudden decrease in specific conductance seen in early to mid October was likely due in part to the end of irrigation season (April 1st to September 30th). (Figure 10). This drop in specific conductance corresponds to an increase in stream discharge for the same period (USGS #14046500 at Service Creek). Figure 11 shows the data rating/grade for each deployment period (monthly interval). These standard USGS ratings are based on the degree of sensor fouling and drift encountered during each deployment period (Wagner et al. 2006; Starkey et al. 2008). Specific conductance data grades less than excellent were due to a combination of fouling and sensor drift.

  Corrections applied to the specific conductance data are listed in Appendix E.

- *Total Dissolved Solids (TDS):*
  Average total dissolved solids was 210 mg/L and never exceeded the regulatory threshold of 500 mg/L. Data rating/grades for each deployment period (monthly interval) are the same as for specific conductance (Figure 12).

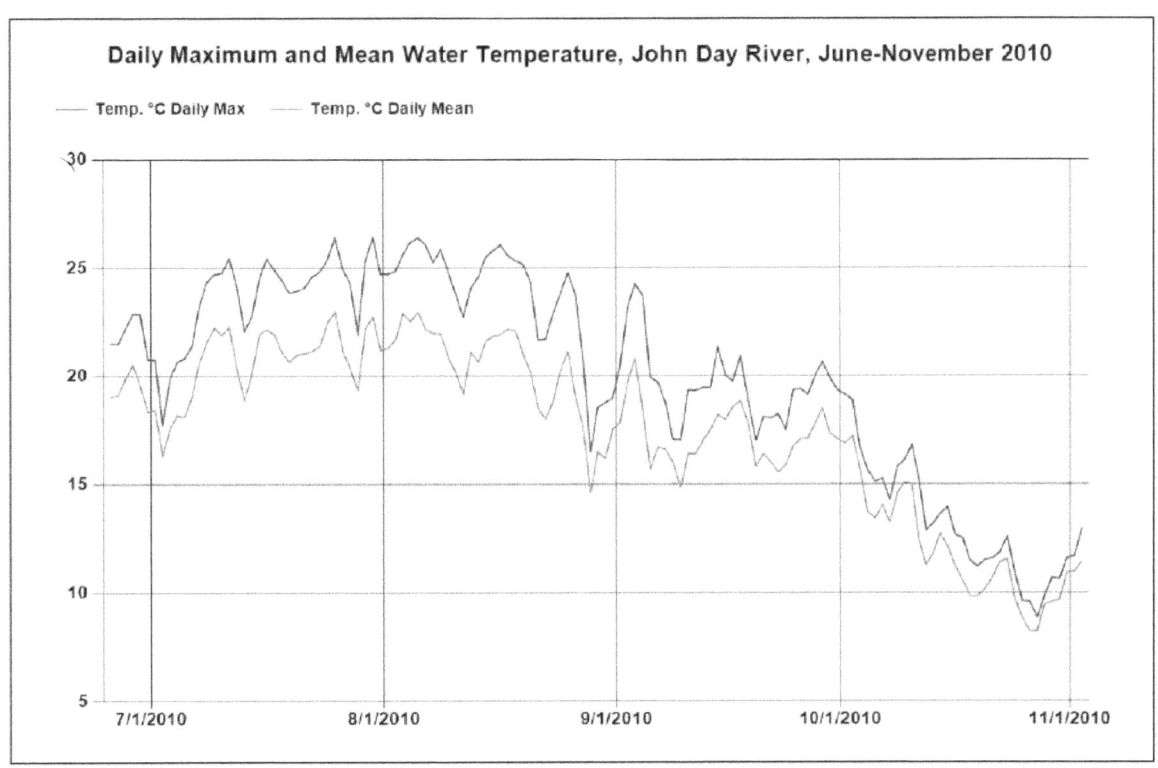

Figure 8. Daily maximum and mean temperature in the John Day River, JODA, 2010.

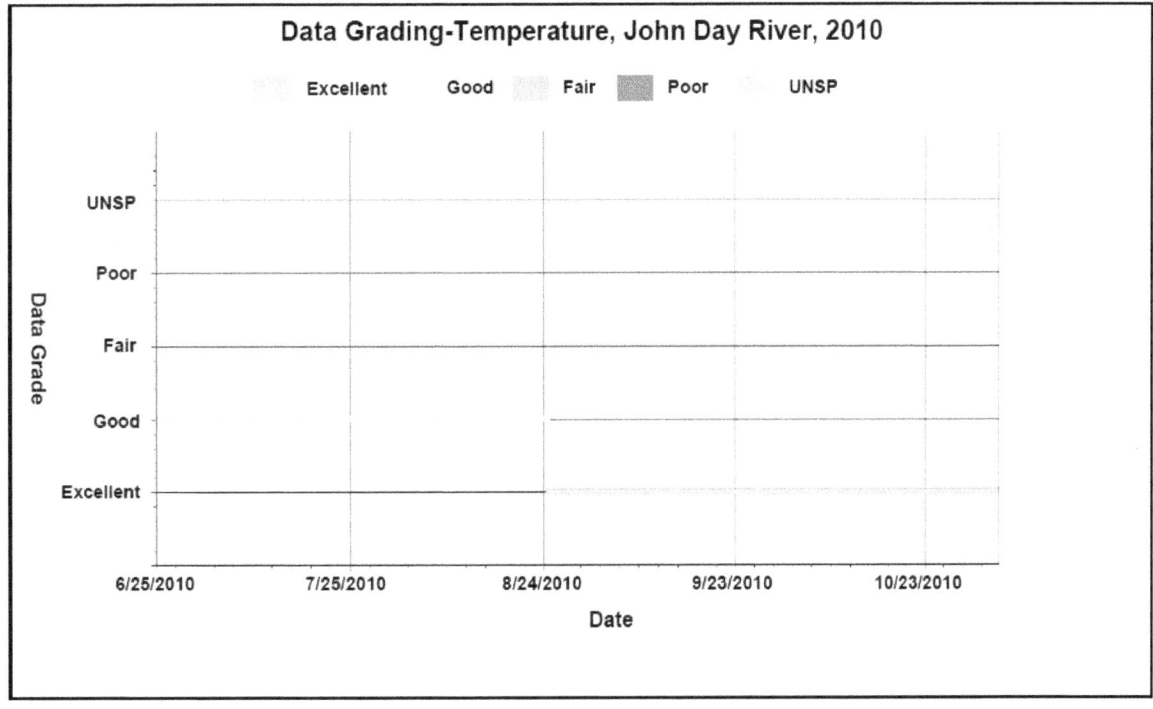

Figure 9. Data grade/rating for temperature each deployment period June-November in the John Day River, JODA, 2010.

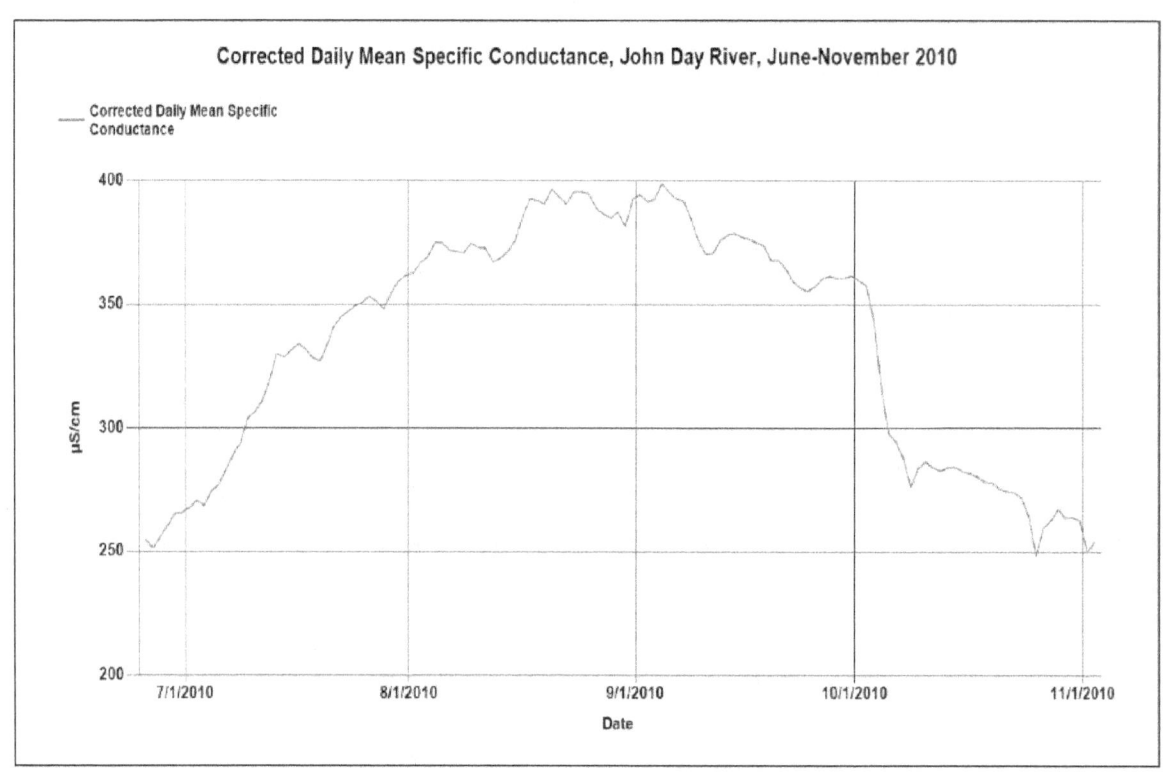

Figure 10. Corrected daily mean specific conductance in the John Day River, JODA, 2010.

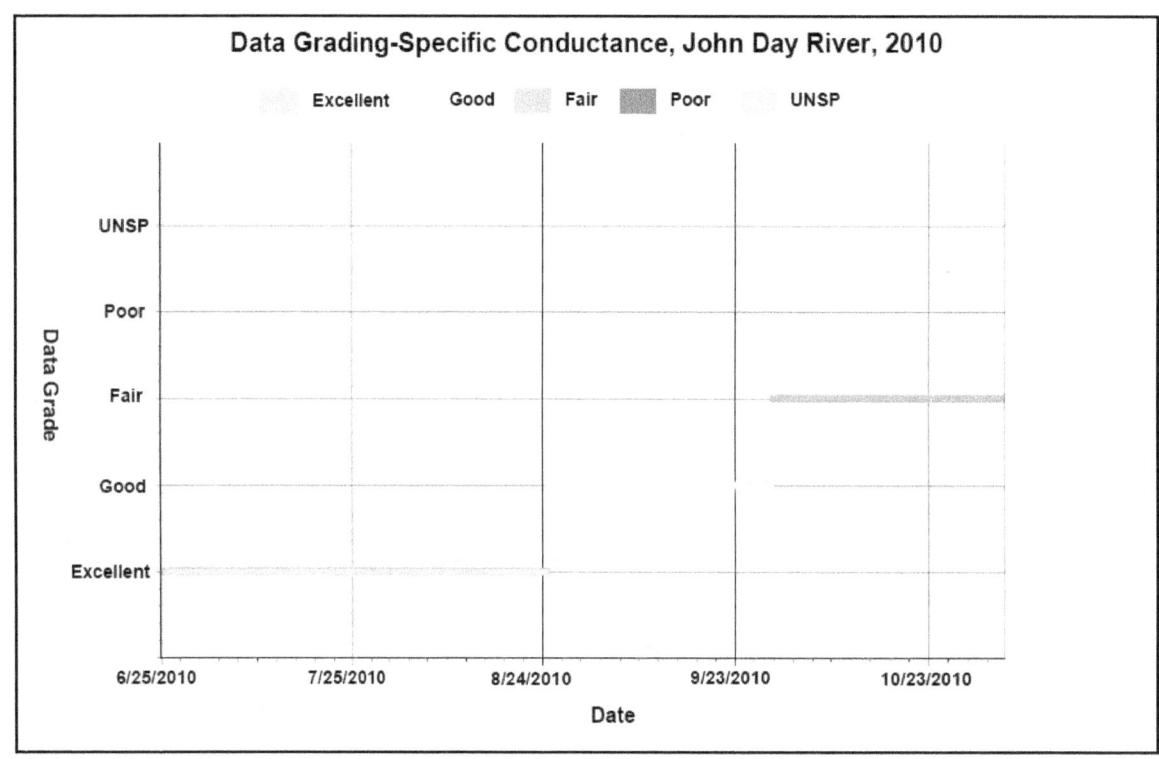

Figure 11. Data grade/rating for specific conductance each deployment period June-November in the John Day River, JODA, 2010.Note that a data grades "good" and "fair" were primarily due to sensor fouling.

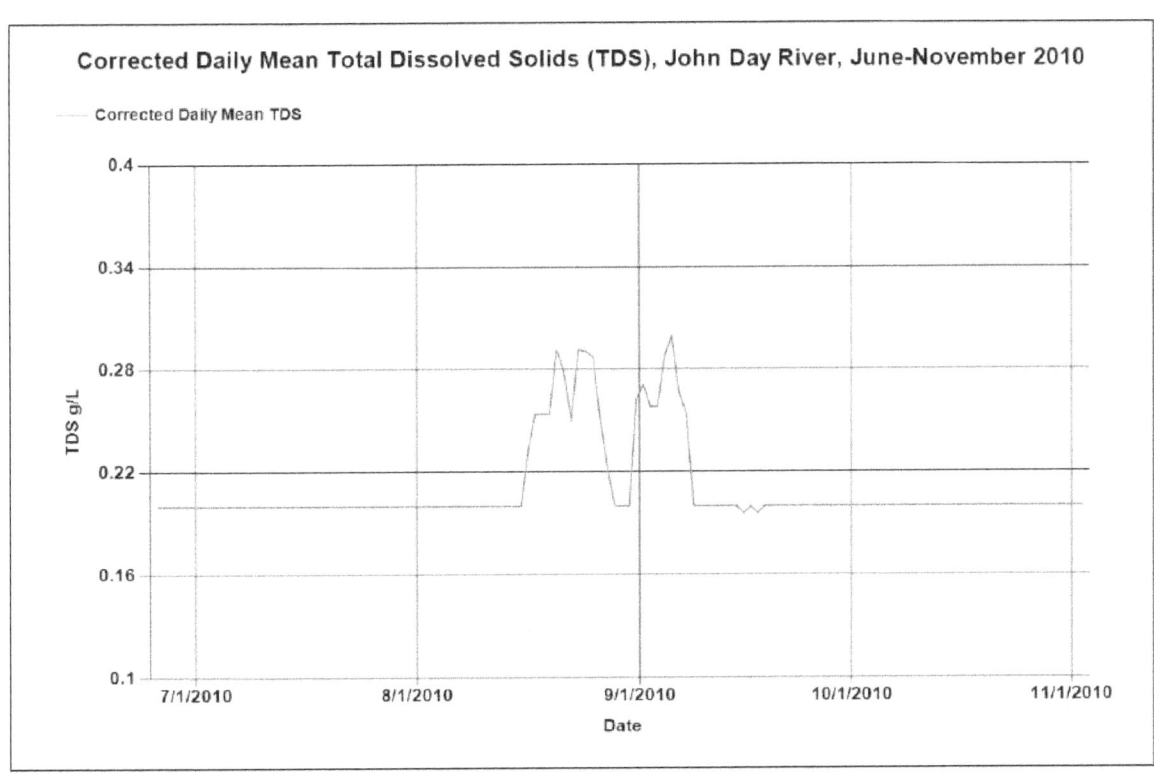

Figure 12. Corrected daily mean total dissolved solids (TDS) in the John Day River, JODA, 2010. Note that TDS is reported in g/L and state thresholds are generally reported in mg/L. Data grades/ratings for each deployment are the same as for specific conductance (Figure 11).

- *Dissolved Oxygen:*

  Mean daily minimum dissolved oxygen was 7.7 mg/L and dipped below the regulatory threshold (6.5 mg/L) during 56 of the 3,146 observations (0.02%). As expected, low dissolved oxygen levels generally corresponded to spikes in water temperature. Figure 13 shows the daily minimum dissolved oxygen and maximum temperatures in the John Day River from June-November 2010. Figure 14 shows the data rating/grade for each deployment period (monthly interval). These standard USGS ratings are based on the degree of sensor fouling and drift encountered during each deployment period (Wagner et al. 2006; Starkey et al. 2008). "Fair" data grades were primarily due to sensor fouling. Corrections applied to the dissolved oxygen data are listed in Appendix E.

  While the John Day River is listed as impaired for dissolved oxygen, our monitoring indicates that within the park, levels infrequently dipped below the regulatory threshold. However, even infrequent low dissolved oxygen can be a threat to salmonids, especially when coupled with elevated water temperatures. Minimum dissolved oxygen levels can likely be increased if water temperatures are reduced via stream shading and increased base flow. This will require basin-wide riparian and in stream flow improvements in cooperation with other agencies, stakeholders, and adjacent landowners.

- *pH:*

  The minimum and maximum pH (7.83 and 8.85 respectively) were never outside the acceptable regulatory thresholds of 6.5-9.0 pH units and the mean (8.35 pH units) was well within this range. Figure 15 shows the daily maximum, minimum, and mean pH in the John Day River from June-November 2010. Figure 16 shows the data rating/grade for each deployment period (monthly interval). These standard USGS ratings are based on the degree of sensor fouling and drift encountered during each deployment period (Wagner et al. 2006; Starkey et al. 2008). The data grade of "good" was due to a combination of sensor fouling and drift. Corrections applied to the pH data are listed in Appendix E.

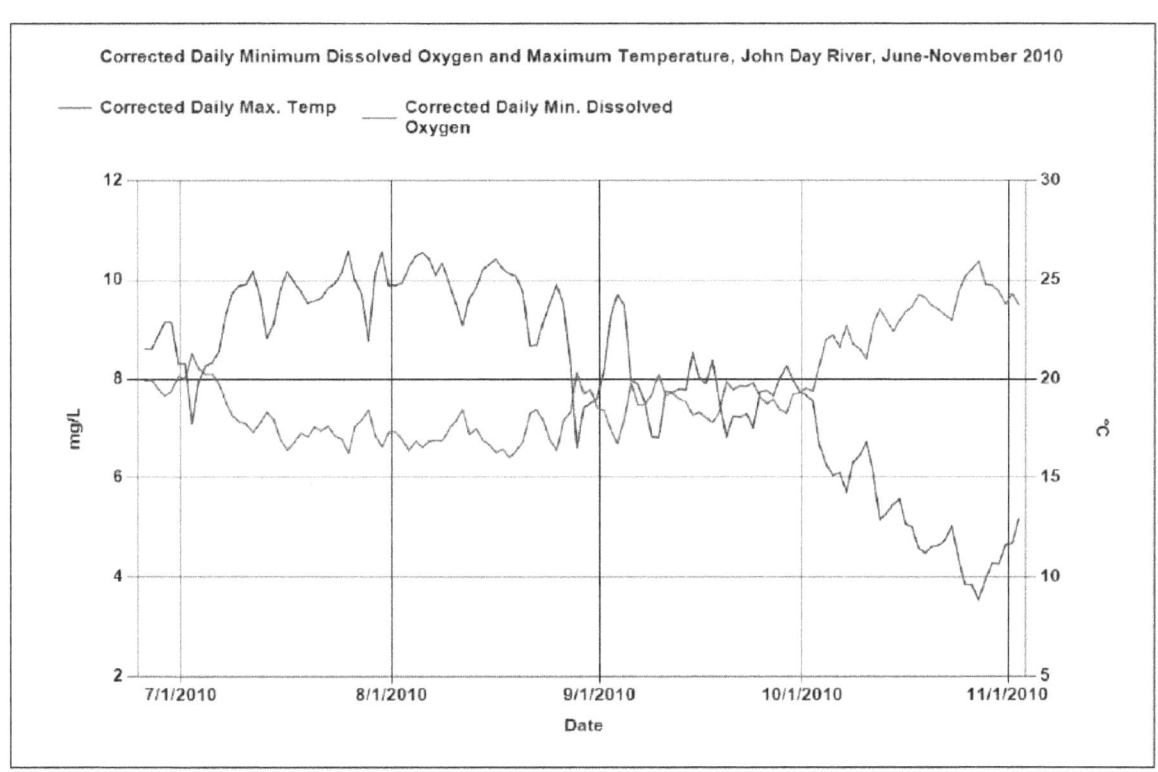

Figure 13. Corrected daily minimum dissolved oxygen and daily maximum temperature in the John Day River, JODA, 2010.

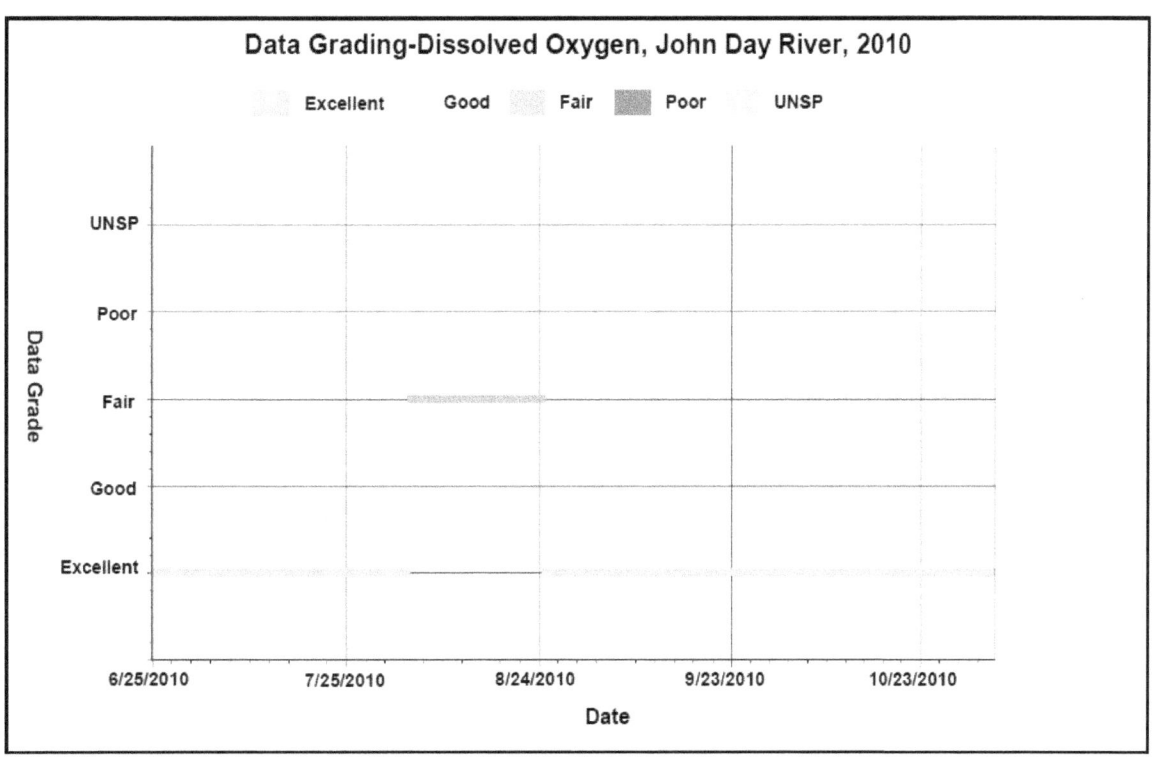

Figure 14. Data grade/rating for dissolved oxygen each deployment period June-November in the John Day River, JODA, 2010.

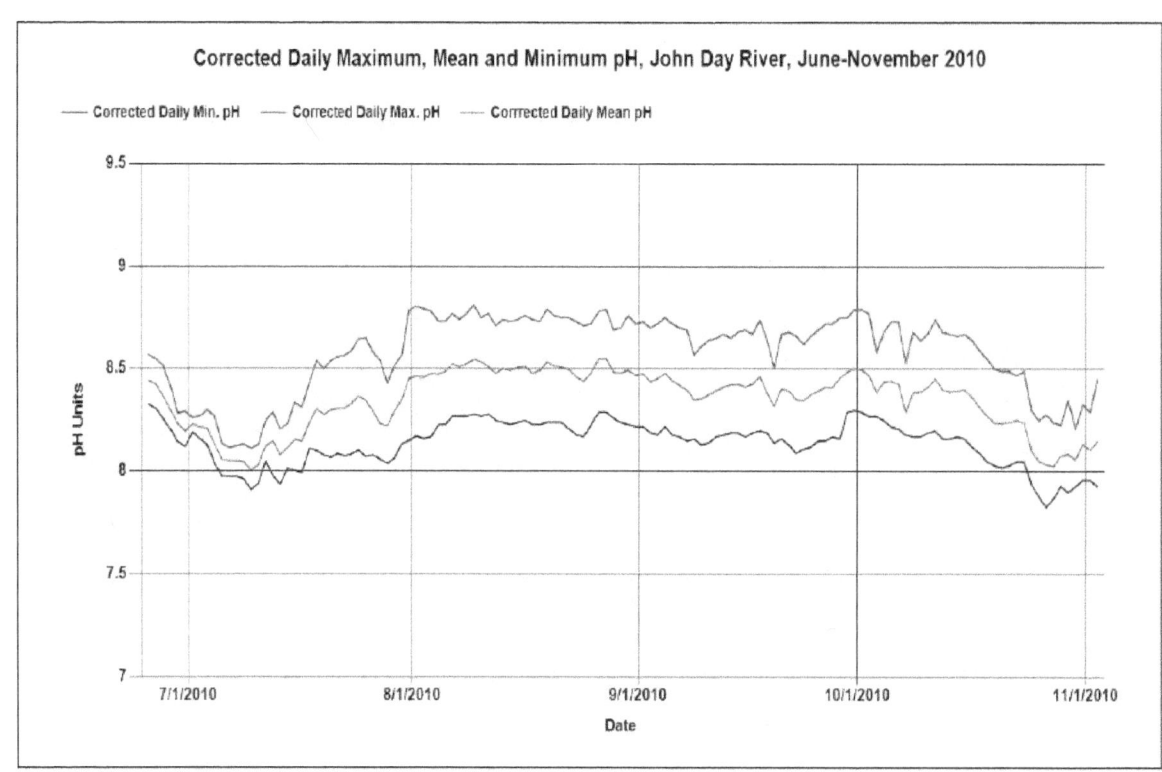

Figure 15. Corrected daily maximum, minimum, and mean pH in the John Day River, JODA, 2010.Note that the maximum and minimum regulatory thresholds were never exceeded (6.5, 9.0 pH units).

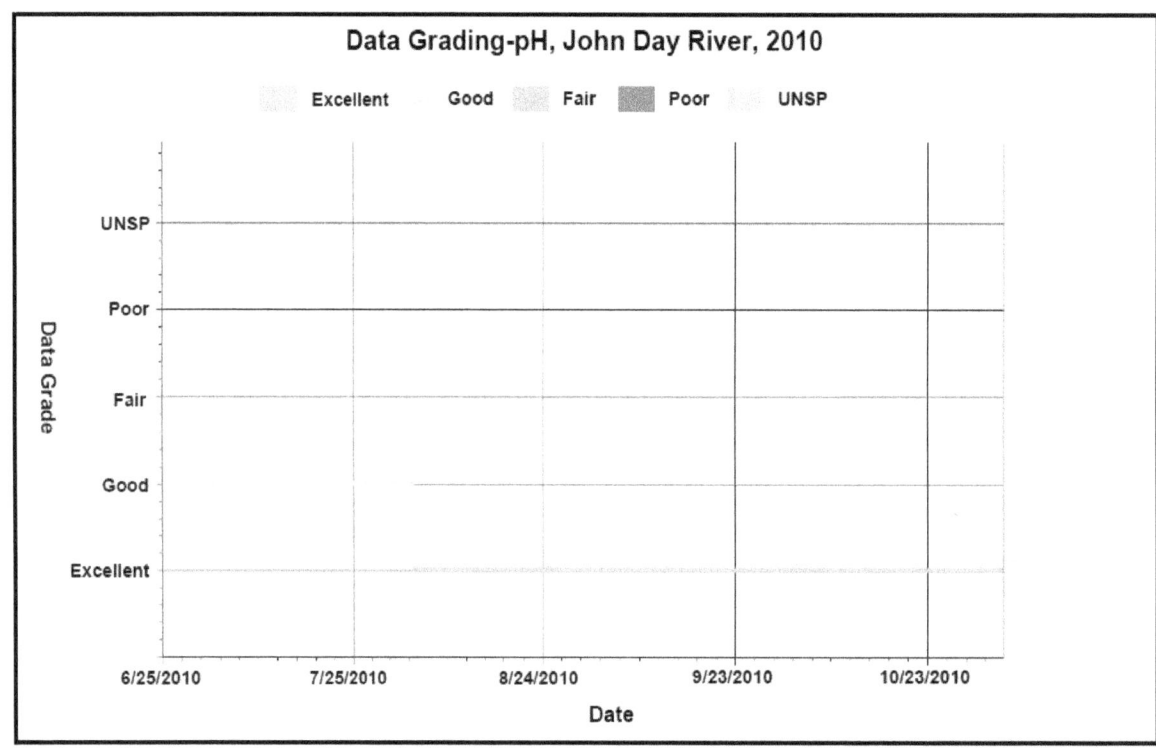

Figure 16. Data grade/rating for pH each deployment period June-November in the John Day River, JODA, 2010.Note that the data grade of "good" was due to a combination of sensor fouling and drift.

- *Turbidity:*

  Prior to discussion about turbidity in the John Day River, it should be noted that conclusions based on this data are limited due to marginal data quality (Figure 18). Sensor fouling due to sediment was the primary factor influencing data quality. It is important to note that the method detection limit (MDL) for this sensor is 0.2 NTU and the minimum level of quantitation (ML) is 0.78 NTU (Appendix D). Figure 17 shows the daily maximum turbidity in the John Day River from June-November 2010. Corrections applied to turbidity data are listed in Appendix E.

  Data indicates that turbidity ranged from 0 to 215 NTU. However, due to poor data quality and lack of historic data for this site the UCBN is unable to determine if conditions exceeded the TMDL. Regulatory thresholds for turbidity state that "< 10% cumulative increase in natural stream turbidities may be allowed, as measured relative to a control point immediately upstream of the turbidity causing activity." Although conclusions are limited based on the quality of data collected in 2010 it is likely that the John Day River does experience relatively high levels of turbidity and sediment load following rain events. It is important to note that the "DEQ is in the process of developing quantitative methods and benchmarks to evaluate sedimentation impairment in Oregon streams" (OR DEQ 2010).

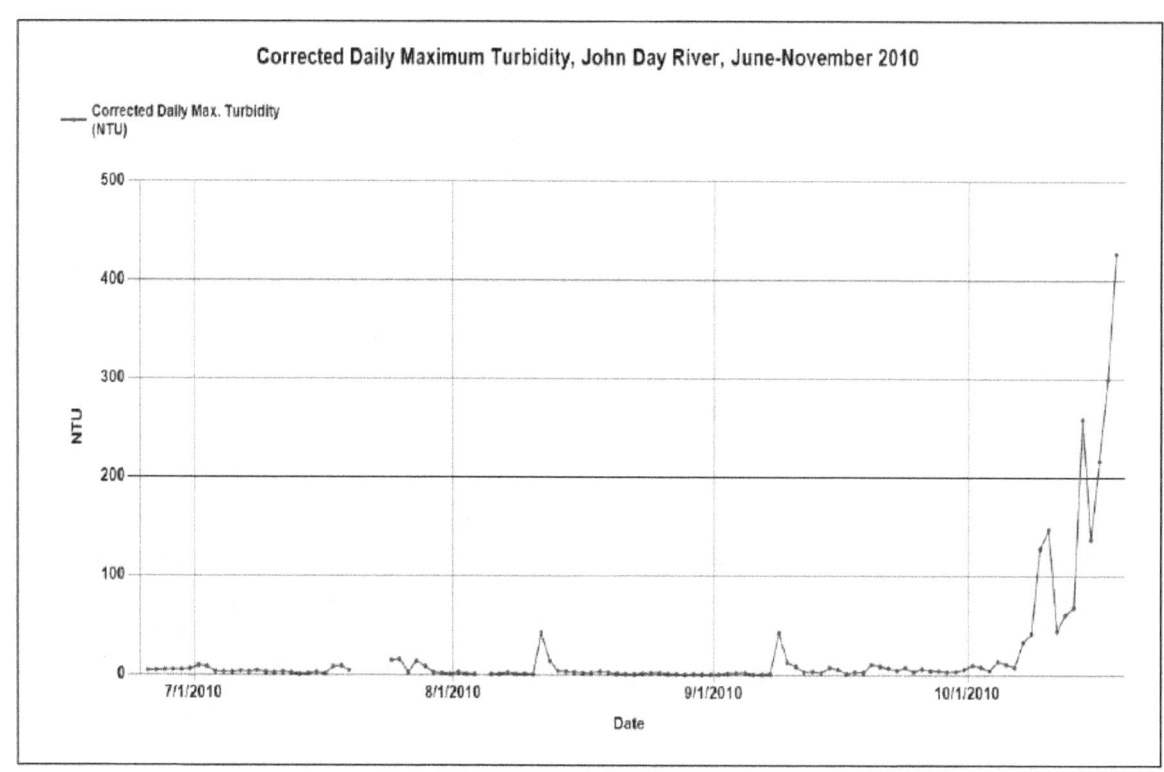

Figure 17. Corrected daily maximum turbidity in the John Day River, JODA, 2010.Note that the un-usable data grades (blue) presented in Figure 18 were primarily due to severe fouling.

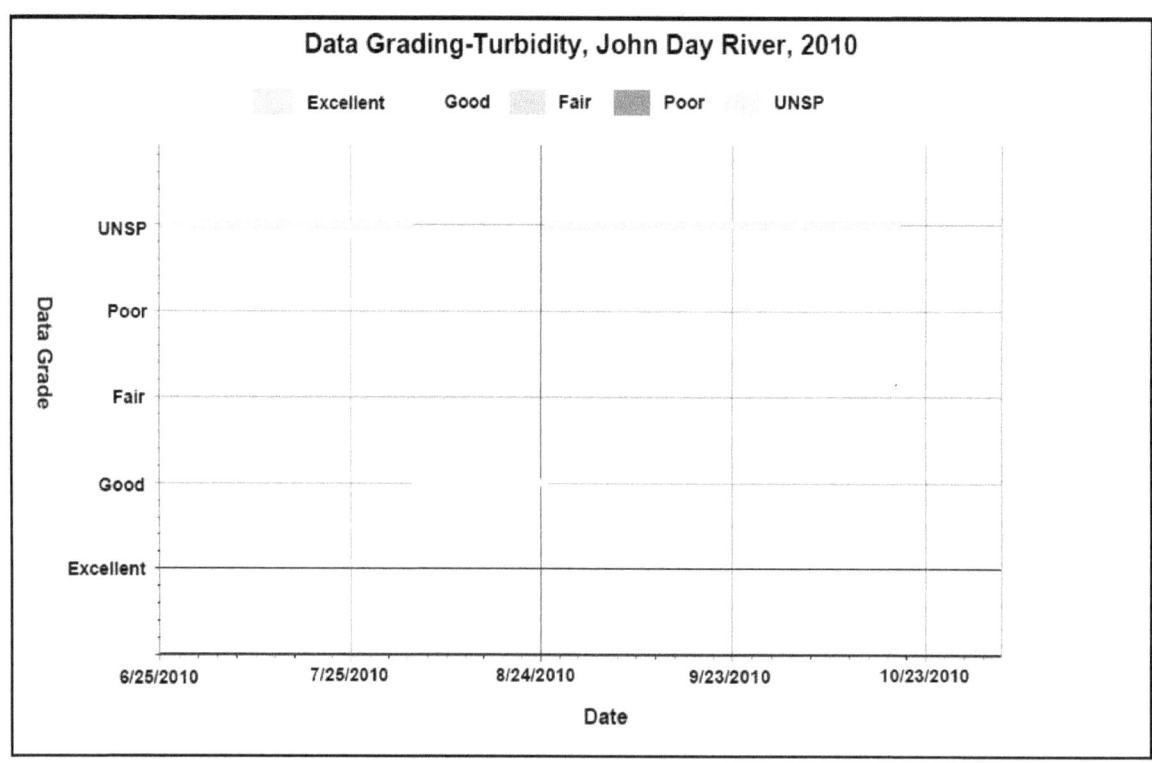

Figure 18. Data grade/rating for turbidity each deployment period June-November in the John Day River, JODA, 2010.Un-usable data ratings (blue) were primarily due to severe fouling.

Macroinvertebrates

Status:

The Hilsenhoff Biotic Index (HBI), which summarizes pollution tolerances of the macroinvertebrate taxa within the sample, ranged from 3.24 to 4.85 with a mean of 3.93. The mean HBI value indicates that the segment of John Day River within the park has "possible slight organic pollution" (Hilsenhoff 1987, 1988). HBI values generally increase (HBI ranges from 0.0 to 10.0) as nutrient enrichment increases. While HBI is most sensitive to organic pollution, it may also respond to sediment loading, low dissolved oxygen and elevated water temperatures. The US Forest Service (USFS) community tolerance quotient ranged from 68 to 79 and indicates that the John Day River's benthic macroinvertebrate community is somewhat impaired. Values of the USFS tolerance quotient range from 20 to just over100, with lower values indicating better water quality.

The median number of Ephemeroptera, Plecoptera, Trichoptera (EPT) taxa was 16.5; the median number of long lived taxa was 5; and the dominate family in 3 of the 6 samples was Heptageniidae (flat-headed mayflies). In the other 3 samples, the dominate family was Baetidae (2 samples) and Simulidae (1 sample). These data along with the tolerance indices listed above suggest that this segment of the John Day River is somewhat impaired. Causes of impairment may be tied to elevated water temperatures, low dissolved oxygen levels, or physical factors such as substrate armoring. See the 2011 stream channel characteristics and riparian condition monitoring annual report for more information about physical factors that may be influencing macroinvertebrate assemblages in the John Day River (Starkey 2011).

The observed to expected ratio (OE) for these samples ranged from 0.35 to 0.45 and indicated that the John Day River was in "poor" condition. However, due to physiographic and climatic conditions at the sample location the model had to extrapolate rather than interpolate predictor variables. As a result the condition rating should be interpreted with caution. See Table 2 and Appendix F for additional summary metrics.

Another finding of interest to the park is that no crayfish in the genus *Pacifastacus* were found this genus includes the native signal crayfish (*Pacificastacus leniusculus*). While relatively low in abundance within the samples, crayfish in the genus *Orconectes* were found in 2 of the 6 samples. The genus *Orconectes* includes rustry crayfish but the specimines were too small for identification to species (i.e. could not confirm they were rusty crayfish). For more information about rusty crayfish in the John Day River see Olden et al. 2009.

Table 2. Vital sign summary table for benthic macroinvertebrates in John Day River, 2010.

PIBO Station	John Day River Macroinvertebrate Summary August 2010					
	3073	**3074**	**3075**	**3076**	**3077**	**3078**
Sample ID	**146650**	**146651**	**146652**	**146653**	**146654**	**146655**
Richness*	22	31	29	22	23	28
Shannon's Diversity*	2.45	2.93	2.83	2.47	1.88	2.72
Simpson's Diversity*	0.89	0.93	0.93	0.87	0.74	0.92
Evenness*	0.79	0.85	0.84	0.80	0.60	0.82
# of EPT Taxa*	11	19	18	13	15	18
Dominant Family	Heptageniidae	Heptageniidae	Heptageniidae	Baetidae	Simuliidae	Baetidae
Dominant Taxa	Simulium	Heptageniidae	Heptageniidae	Orthocladiinae	Simulium	Baetis
Hilsenhoff Biotic Index*	4.24	3.26	3.24	4.24	4.85	3.72
# of Intolerant Taxa*	1	5	6	4	5	6
# of Tolerant Taxa*	0	0	0	0	1	0
USFS Community						
Tolerance Quotient (d)*	79	72	68	78	77	71
# of shredder taxa*	1	1	1	1	0	1
# of scraper taxa*	2	2	6	2	2	2
# of collector-filterer taxa*	3	4	4	2	3	3
# of collector-gatherer taxa*	8	13	9	9	9	13
# of predator taxa*	2	4	5	4	5	4
# of clinger taxa*	10	12	13	8	9	11
Long-lived Taxa*	5	5	5	4	5	6

Coliform

Status:

The coliform sample from Picture Gorge indicates that in late August the John Day River fell well below the TMDL for *E. coli* (individual sample < 406 *E. coli*/100 ml) with a concentration of 9 MPN/100 ml (Table 3). In comparison, the OR DEQ John Day River basin TMDL-bacteria assessment indicates that between June 2005 and April 2006 *E. coli* concentrations in Picture Gorge (station #28452) ranged from 13-291 organisms/100 ml with a median concentration of 40 organisms/100 ml (Appendix E OR DEQ 2010). Maximum concentrations occurred in summer and fall seasons.

Our samples relatively low concentration may be attributed to low stream flow and lack of recent rainfall/surface flow.

JODA should consider monthly evaluation of *E. coli* during peak visitor use due to the primary contact recreation (primarily fishing) that occurs in the river. Given that the park already conducts routine coliform sampling of its drinking water, occasional samples of stream water during the summer would be relatively easy to obtain. Monthly samples would also help establish a baseline to which future samples can be compared.

Table 3. Results of coliform samples taken from the John Day River in August 2010.

Sample Date	Location	Total Coliform	Fecal Coliform	*E. coli*
8/25/2010	John Day River, Picture Gorge- near old USGS gage.	830 MPN/100 ml	10 /100 ml	9 MPN/100 ml

MPN= most probable number

Bridge Creek- Painted Hills Unit

Water Chemistry:

Cross Section Survey:
A cross section survey was conducted at the proposed multiprobe deployment location to evaluate if the site was reasonably representative of stream conditions throughout the park. As suggested by the water resource division the UCBN judges overall representativeness primarily on the basis of specific conductance (Starkey et al. 2008).

The 2010 deployment location provided adequate water depth throughout the field season, was easily accessible, and was away from heavily trafficked access points.

A one way analysis of variance (ANOVA) test was conducted to evaluate representativeness (R v2.12.0). Results of the ANOVA showed that there was a significant difference for specific conductance among the transects and the deployment location in August $F(4,40)= 7.97$, $p< 0.001$ and a significant difference in November $F(4,38)= 5.06$, $p < 0.001$ (Figures 19 and 20).

To determine where the difference in representativeness occurred, a post hoc Tukey's test was conducted (R v2.12.0). Relative to specific conductance, results of the Tukey's test for the cross section conducted in August indicates that the deployment location was significantly different from transect 2. Results of the Tukey's test for the cross section conducted in November indicates that the deployment location was significantly different from transect 3.

In summary, the deployment location was representative of the majority of upstream transects, and results do not indicate a need to move the water quality multiprobe for future sampling.

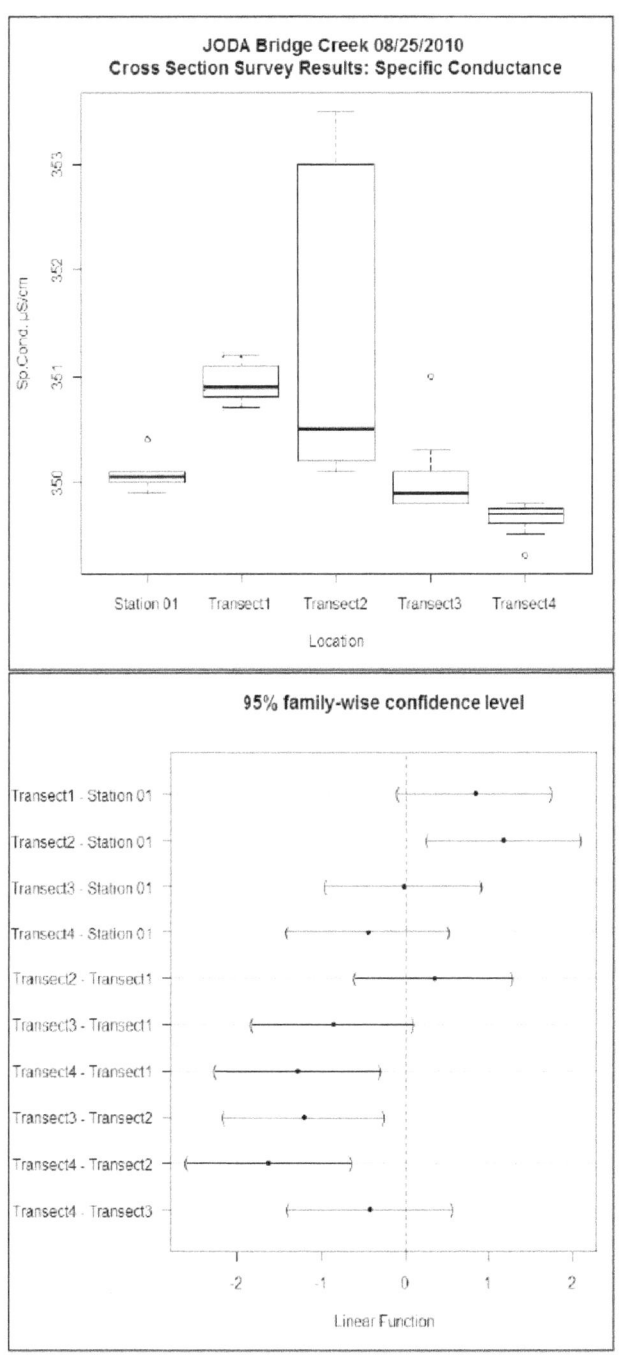

Figure 19. August 2010 cross section survey of Bridge Creek, box plot of specific conductance and plot of 95% family-wise confidence level.Note that "Station 01" is the location of multiprobe deployment and the transects progress upstream (1-4).

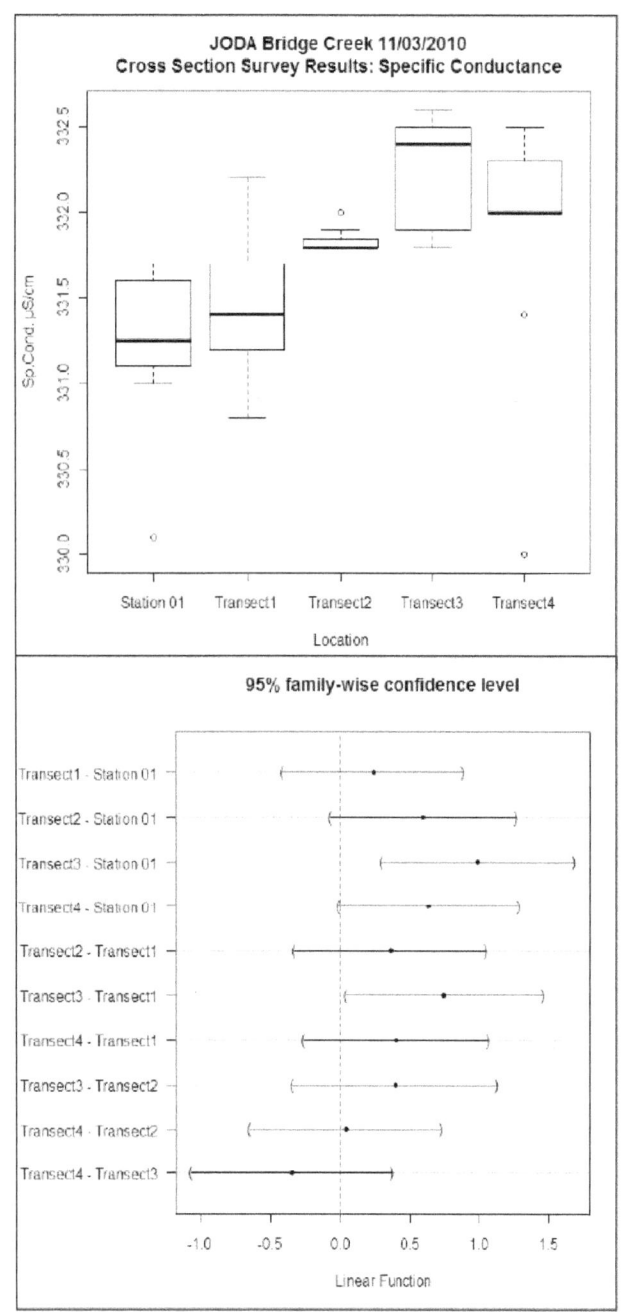

Figure 20. November 2010 cross section survey of Bridge Creek, box plot of specific conductance and plot of 95% family-wise confidence level.Note that "Station 01" is the location of multiprobe deployment and the transects progress upstream (1-4).

Status:

Condition of core water quality parameters along with the corresponding state Department of Environmental Quality (DEQ) regulatory threshold are given in Table 4. As in the John Day River, the primary concern in Bridge Creek is elevated water temperatures and their effect on native salmonids.

Table 4. Vital sign summary table for water chemistry in Bridge Creek June-November, 2010.

Bridge Creek Water Chemistry Summary 2010

Measure	Current Condition (June-November, 2010)	State DEQ Thresholds	% Exceedance[a]
Temperature (*MDMT, **MDAT)	* MDMT= 23.57 °C ** MDAT= 19.78 °C	7 day average < 18 °C (salmon/trout rearing/migration)	12.5 %
Total dissolved solids /TDS (mean)	200 mg/L	TDS < 500 mg/L	0 %
Dissolved oxygen (mean daily min)	8.70 mg/L	> 6.5 mg/L instantaneous (cool water, non-spawning)	0 %
pH (mean daily max)	8.54 pH Units	9.0 pH Units	< 1 %
pH (mean daily min)	8.22 pH Units	6.5 pH Units	0 %
Turbidity (mean daily max)	31.48 NTU	< 10% cumulative increase in natural stream turbidities may be allowed, as measured relative to a control point immediately upstream of the turbidity causing activity	Insufficient data
E. coli	220 MPN/100 ml	< 406 E. coli/100 ml	0 %

*MDMT – Maximum Daily Maximum Temperature **MDAT – Maximum Daily Average Temperature

0-5% exceedance	
5-25% exceedance	
>25% exceedance	

- *Temperature:*
  The 7 day average temperature exceeded 18.0 °C in 12.5% of observations and the maximum daily maximum temperature (MDMT) was 23.6 °C. Our data reinforces basin-wide temperature concerns as discussed in the John Day River Basin Total Maximum Daily Load (TMDL) and Water Quality Management Plan (OR DEQ 2010). Figure 21 shows the daily maximum and mean daily temperatures in Bridge Creek from June-November 2010. Figure 22 shows the data rating/grade for each deployment period (monthly interval). These standard USGS ratings are based on the degree of sensor fouling encountered during each deployment period (Wagner et al. 2006; Starkey et al. 2008). It should be noted that in August, the Hydrolab was removed and sent in for repair of the D.O. sensor. At this time, the HACH Company determined the temperature sensor was slightly outside of acceptance criteria (0.1 °C) and replaced the sensor. This slight sensor error likely contributed to the "good" data grade June-August (Figure 22).

  Water temperatures are of particular interest in Bridge Creek, given that its designated fish use is for salmon and trout rearing and migration (note: includes all salmon species, steelhead, rainbow and cutthroat trout). Elevated water temperatures can be caused by poor stream shading and dewatering. Implications of elevated water temperatures may include decreased salmonid recruitment, decreased salmonid health, and potential shifts in fish and benthic macroinvertebrate communities (Vannote and Sweeney 1980; McCullough 1999).

Maintaining water temperatures suitable for naturally occurring species in Bridge Creek will depend on riparian condition and reduced dewatering. For this reason cooperation with other agencies, stakeholders, and adjacent landowners will be critical for improving water temperature. One example of ongoing cooperation includes extensive riparian restoration throughout much of the Bridge Creek watershed as part of the Intensively Monitored Watershed project implemented by NOAA Fisheries, Northwest Fisheries Science Center. NOAA has worked closely with JODA and played an important role in restoration efforts within the Painted Hills Unit. More information on the intensively monitored restoration of Bridge Creek can be found in Pollock (2007), ISEMP (2009), and Hall et al. (2010).

- *Specific Conductance:*
  Specific conductance ranged from 257.0 to 370.0 µS/cm, with an average specific conductance of 328.2 µS/cm (Figure 23). There is no regulatory threshold for specific conductance but rather a threshold for total dissolved solids (see section below). Figure 24 shows the data rating/grade for each deployment period (monthly interval). These standard USGS ratings are based on the degree of sensor fouling and drift encountered during each deployment period (Wagner et al. 2006; Starkey et al. 2008). Specific conductance data grades less than excellent were due primarily to sensor fouling.

  Corrections applied to the specific conductance data are listed in Appendix E.

- *Total Dissolved Solids (TDS):*
  Average total dissolved solids was 200 mg/L and never exceeded the regulatory threshold of 500 mg/L (Figure 25). Data rating/grades for each deployment period (monthly interval) are the same as for specific conductance (Figure 24).

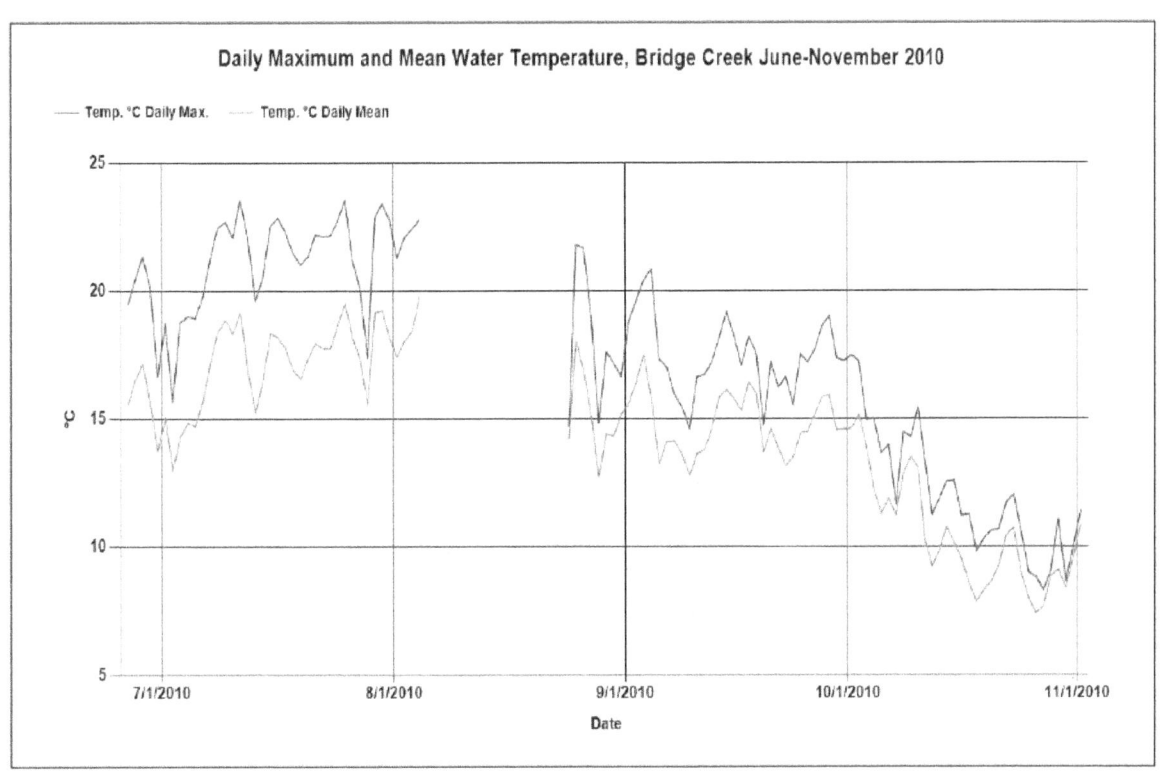

Figure 21. Daily maximum and mean temperature in Bridge Creek, JODA, 2010.

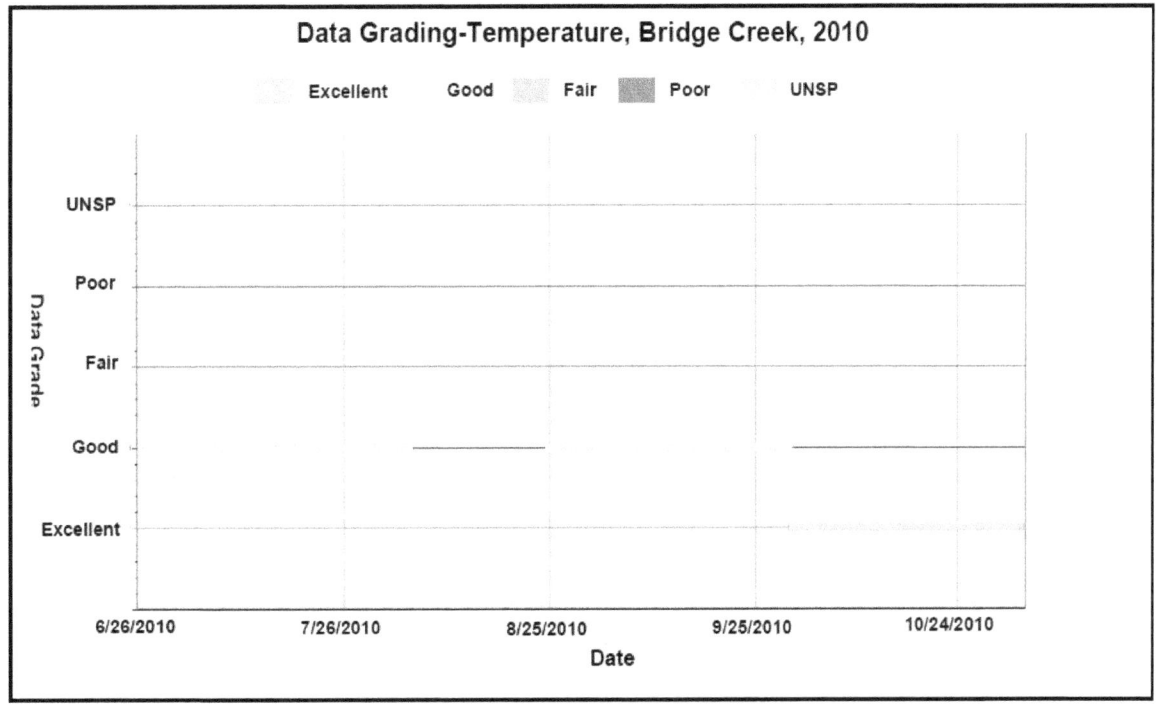

Figure 22. Data grade/rating for temperature each deployment period June-November in Bridge Creek, JODA, 2010.

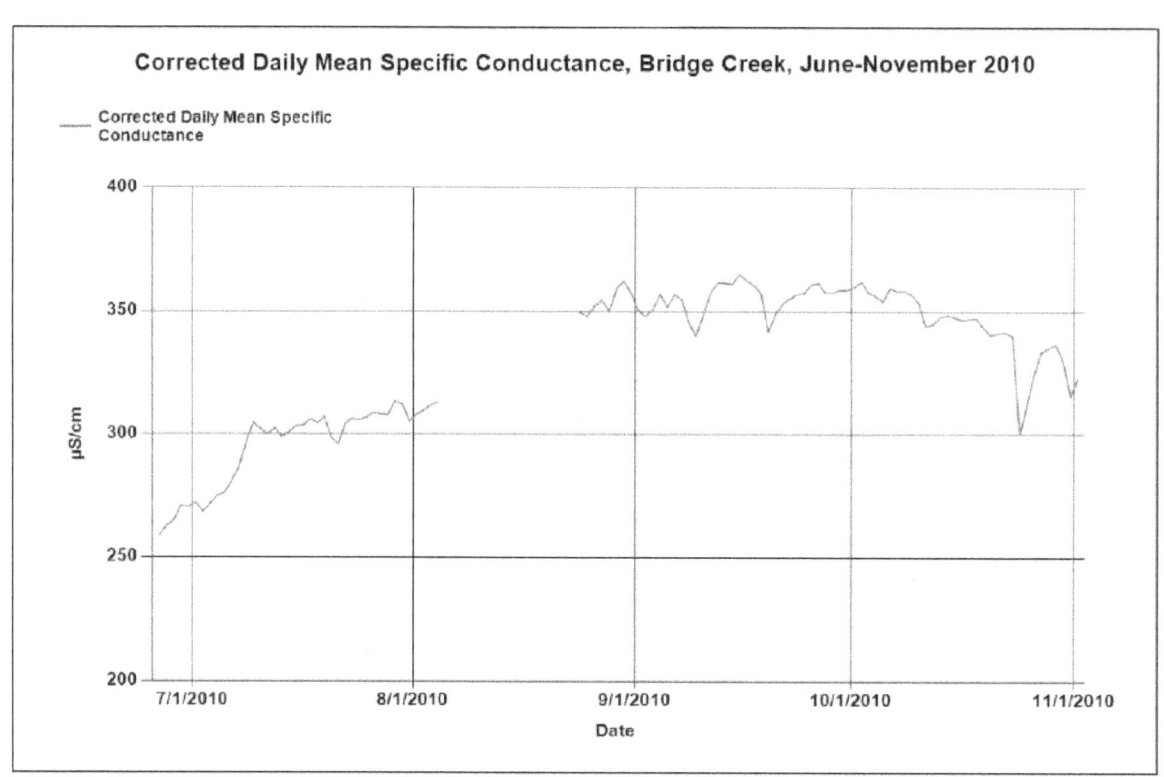

Figure 23. Corrected mean daily specific conductance in Bridge Creek, JODA, 2010.

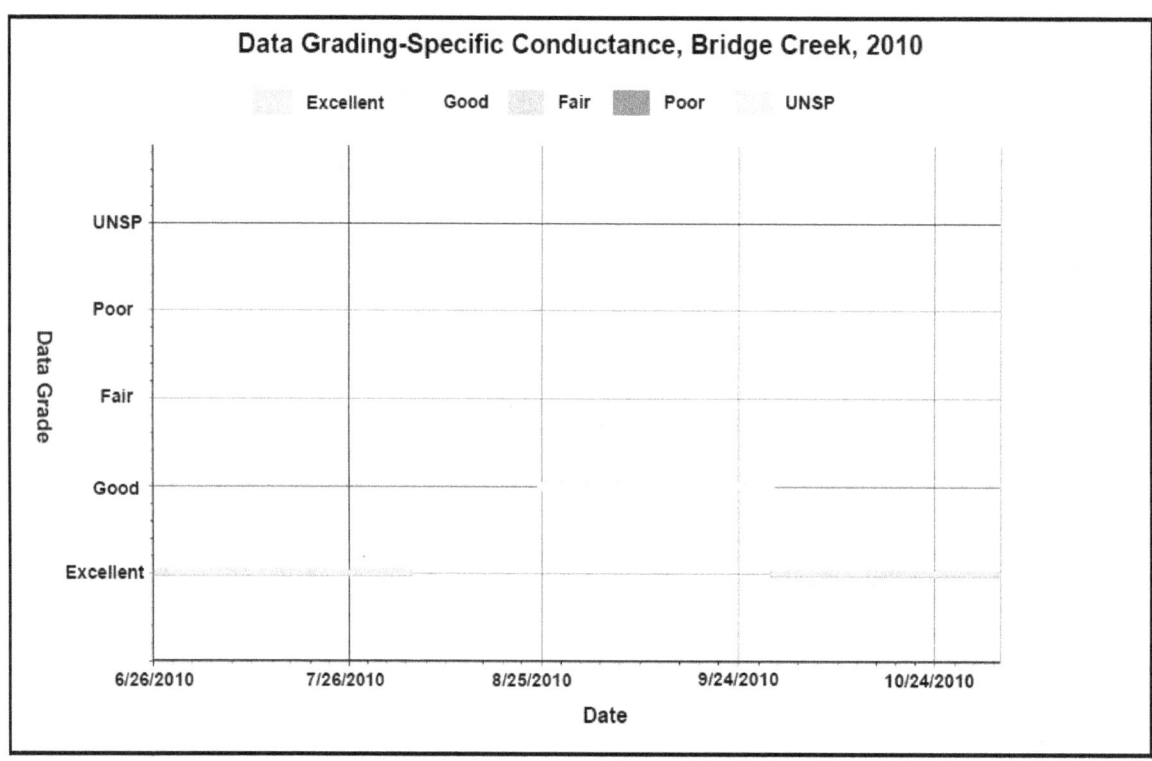

Figure 24. Data grade/rating for specific conductance each deployment period June-November in Bridge Creek, JODA, 2010.Note that a data grade of "good" was primarily due to sensor fouling.

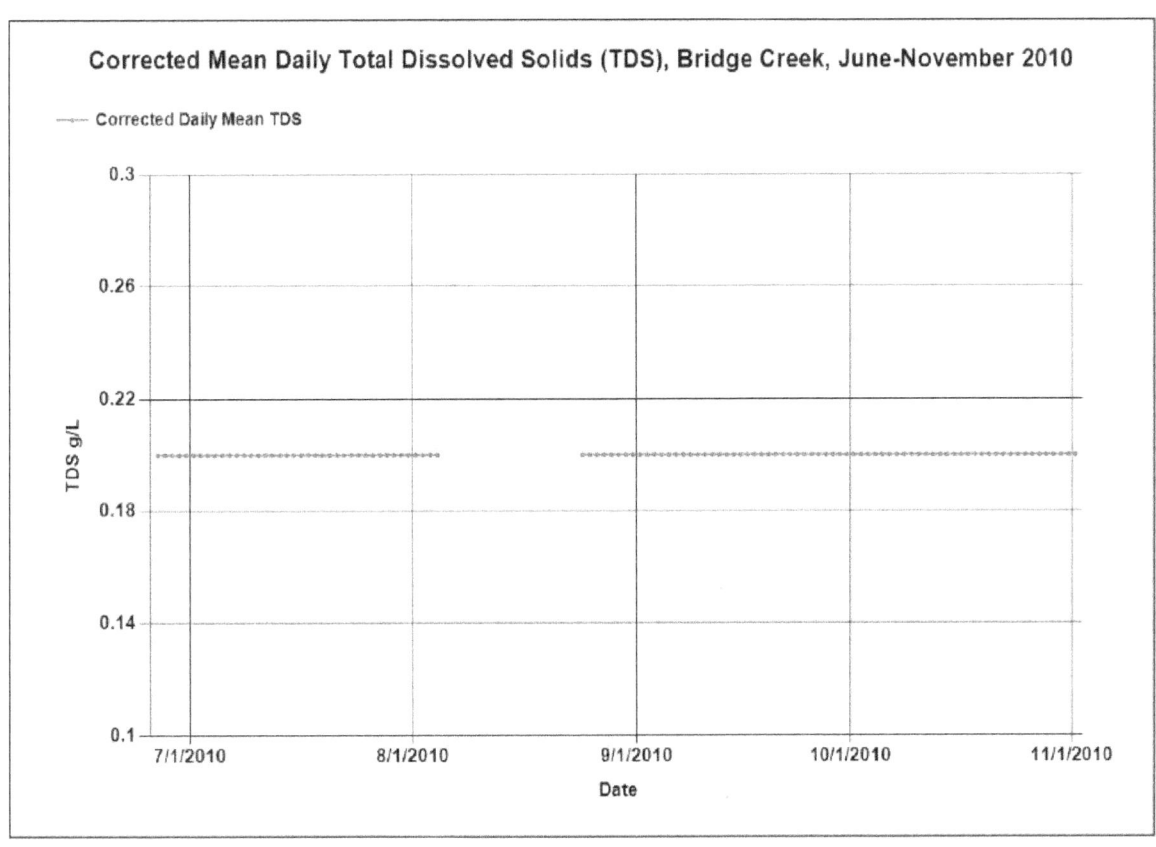

Figure 25. Corrected mean daily total dissolved solids (TDS) in Bridge Creek, JODA, 2010. Note that TDS is reported in g/L and state thresholds are generally reported in mg/L. Data grades/ratings for each deployment are the same as for specific conductance (Figure 24).

- *Dissolved Oxygen:*
Mean daily minimum dissolved oxygen was 8.7 mg/L and never dipped below the regulatory threshold (6.5 mg/L). As expected, the lowest dissolved oxygen levels generally corresponded to spikes in water temperature. Figure 26 shows the daily minimum dissolved oxygen and maximum temperatures in Bridge Creek from June-November 2010. Figure 27 shows the data rating/grade for each deployment period (monthly interval). These standard USGS ratings are based on the degree of sensor fouling and drift encountered during each deployment period (Wagner et al. 2006; Starkey et al. 2008). The "Fair" data grade (October-November) was due to a combination of sensor fouling and drift. Corrections applied to the dissolved oxygen data are listed in Appendix E. Note that in August, the Hydrolab was removed and sent in for repair of the dissolved oxygen sensor and board. Despite the need for repair, data quality during the June-August deployment remained "excellent." This implies sensor/board failure occurred during calibration and not during the deployment.

- *pH:*
The minimum and maximum pH was 7.64 and 9.04 pH units respectively. pH exceeded the upper threshold of 9.0 pH units in 10 of 2,629 observations (0.38%). The lower pH threshold (6.0 pH units) was never exceeded. Figure 28 shows the daily maximum, minimum, and mean pH in Bridge Creek from June-November 2010. Figure 29 shows the data rating/grade for each deployment period (monthly interval). These standard USGS ratings are based on the degree of sensor fouling and drift encountered during each deployment period (Wagner et al. 2006; Starkey et al. 2008). The data grade of "fair" (June-August) was due primarily to sensor drift. Corrections applied to the pH data are listed in Appendix E.

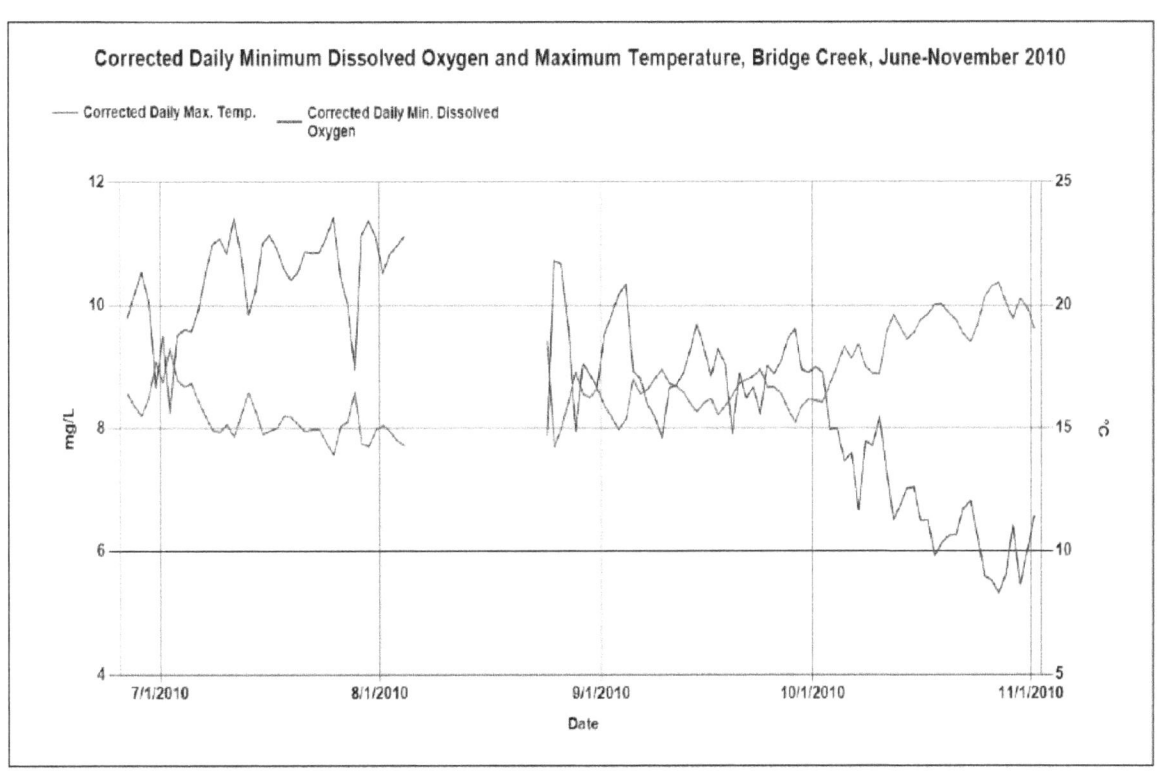

Figure 26. Corrected daily minimum dissolved oxygen and daily maximum temperature in Bridge Creek, JODA, 2010.

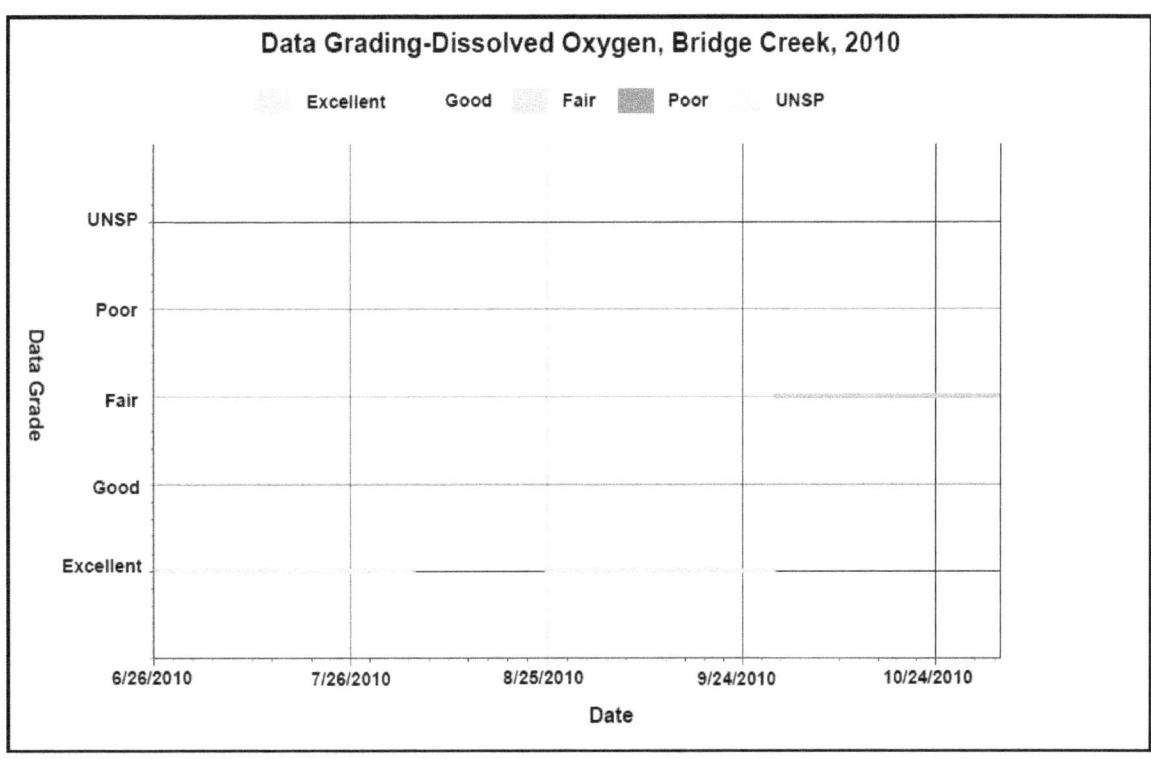

Figure 27. Data grade/rating for dissolved oxygen each deployment period June-November in Bridge Creek, JODA, 2010.

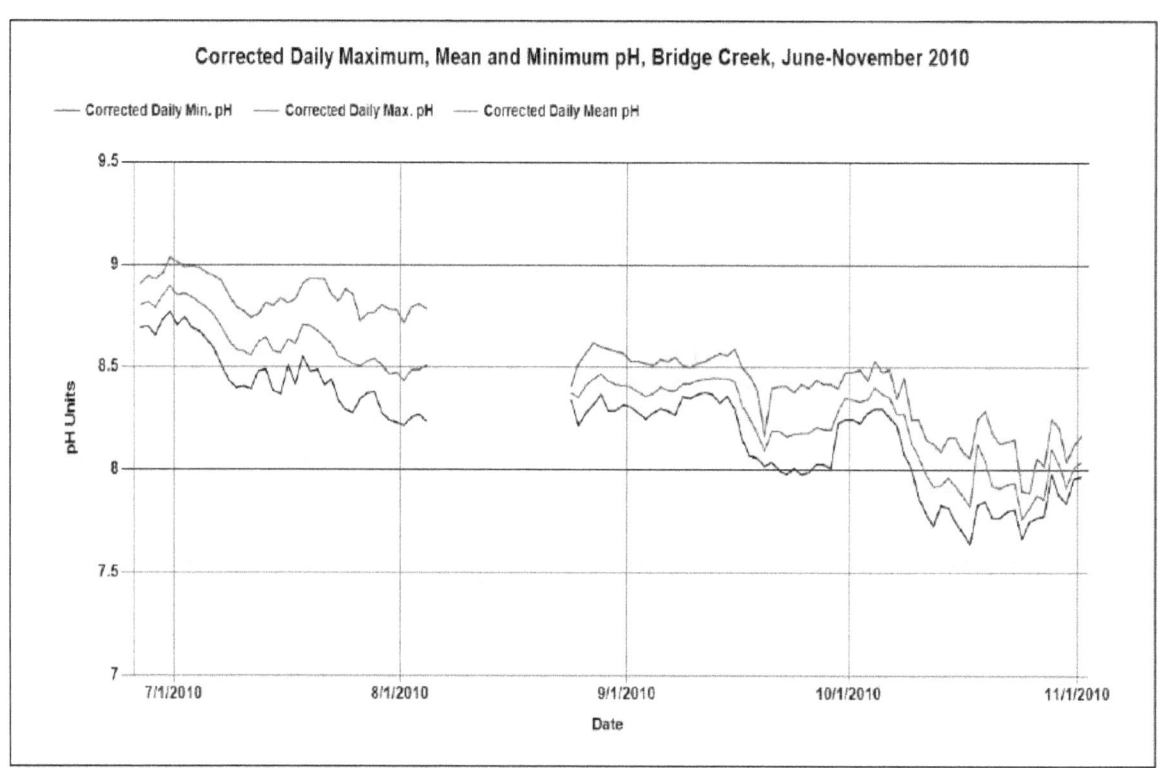

Figure 28. Corrected daily maximum, minimum, and mean pH in Bridge Creek, JODA, 2010.Note that the maximum and minimum regulatory thresholds were never exceeded (6.5, 9.0 pH units)

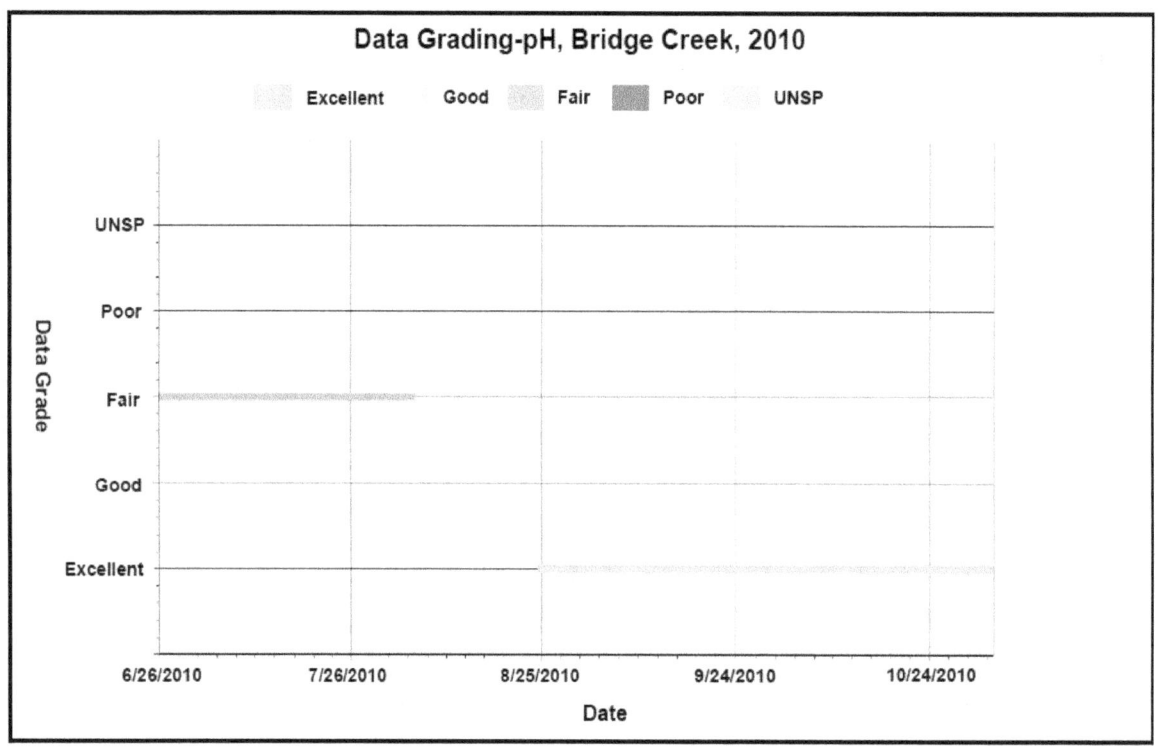

Figure 29. Data grade/rating for pH each deployment period June-November in Bridge Creek, JODA, 2010.Note that the data grade of "fair" was due primarily to sensor drift.

- *Turbidity:*
  Prior to discussion about turbidity in Bridge Creek, it should be noted that conclusions based on this data are limited due to marginal data quality (Figure 31). Sensor fouling due to sediment was the primary factor influencing data quality. It is important to note that the method detection limit (MDL) for this sensor is 0.3 NTU and the minimum level of quantitation (ML) is 0.81 NTU (Appendix D). Figure 30 shows the daily maximum turbidity in Bridge Creek from June-November 2010. Corrections applied to turbidity data are listed in Appendix E.

  Data indicates that turbidity ranged from 0 to 260 NTU. However, due to poor data quality and lack of historic data for this site the UCBN is unable to determine if conditions exceeded the TMDL. Regulatory thresholds for turbidity state that "< 10% cumulative increase in natural stream turbidities may be allowed, as measured relative to a control point immediately upstream of the turbidity causing activity." Although conclusions are limited based on the quality of data collected in 2010 it is likely Bridge Creek does experience relatively high levels of turbidity and sediment load following rain events. This was particularly evident during the September site visit when the multiprobe housing was filled with approximately 4 inches of sediment. It is important to note that the "DEQ is in the process of developing quantitative methods and benchmarks to evaluate sedimentation impairment in Oregon streams" (OR DEQ 2010).

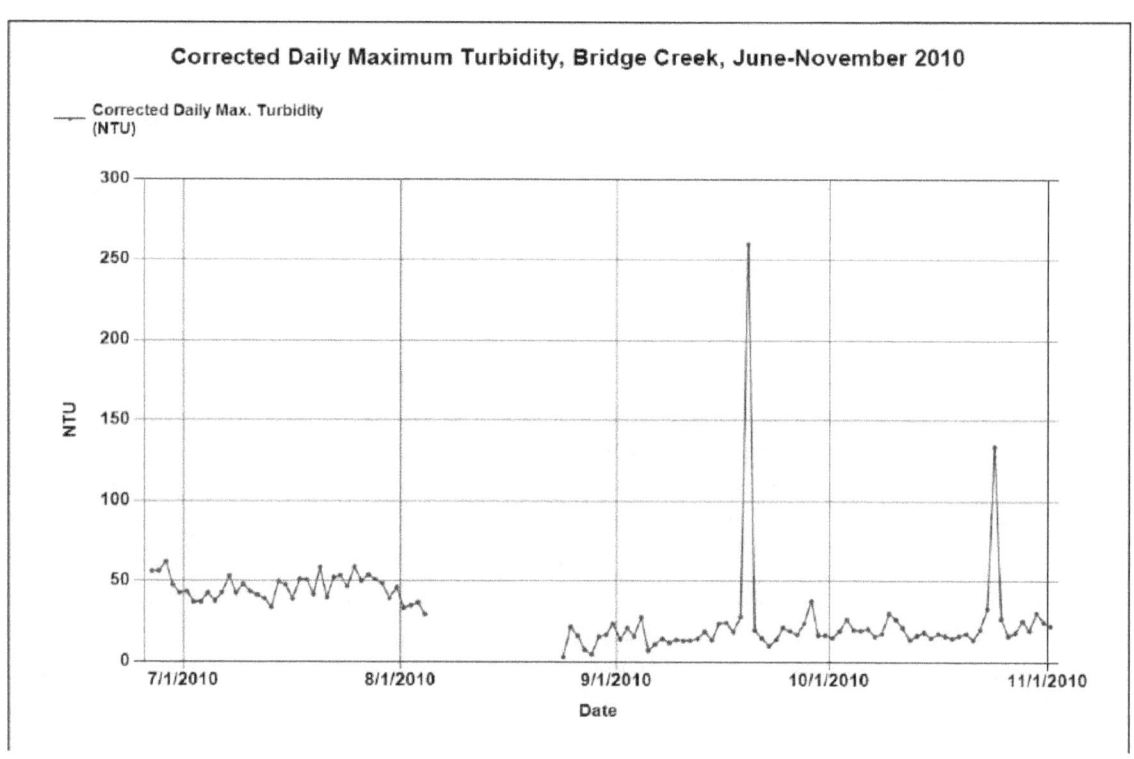

Figure 30. Corrected daily maximum turbidity in Bridge Creek, JODA, 2010.Note that the "un-usable" (blue) and "poor" (red) data grades presented in Figure 31 were primarily due to severe fouling.

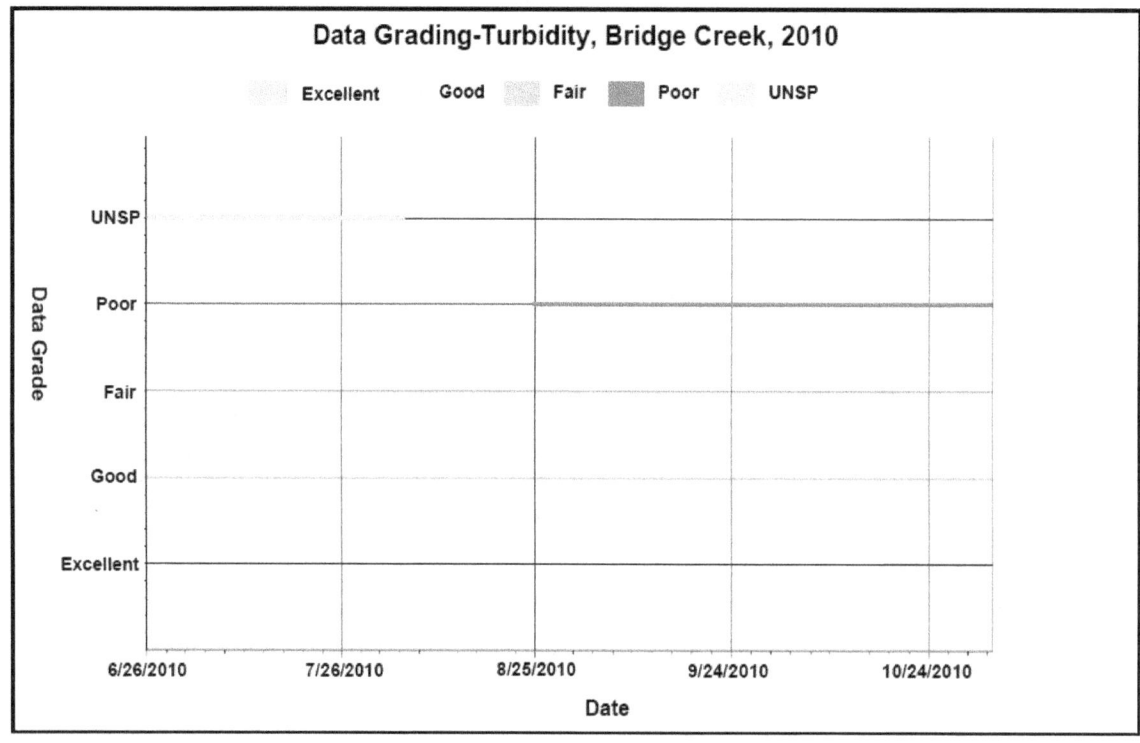

Figure 31. Data grade/rating for turbidity each deployment period June-November in Bridge Creek, JODA, 2010.Note that the "un-usable" (blue) and "poor" (red) data grades were primarily due to severe fouling.

38

Macroinvertebrates

Status:
Due to the extensive monitoring of Bridge Creek by NOAA the UCBN did not collect benthic macroinvertebrates in 2010. The methods used by NOAA to collect macroinvertebrates are based on those used by USFS PACFISH/INFISH Biological Opinion (PIBO) and are outlined in Weber (2009). More information on the intensively monitored restoration of Bridge Creek can be found in Pollock (2007), ISEMP (2009), and Hall et al. (2010).

Coliform

Status:
The coliform sample from Bridge Creek indicates that in late August *E. coli* levels (220 MPN/100 ml) fell below the TMDL for individual samples (< 406 *E. coli*/100 ml) (Table 5). Total coliform was relatively high; however, fecal coliform was well below the previous bacteria standard of 400/100 ml. Note that prior to 1996 fecal coliform was used as the indicator bacteria, the current standard uses *E. coli*.

Table 5. Results of coliform samples taken in the Bridge Creek in August 2010.

Sample Date	Location	Total Coliform	Fecal Coliform	*E. coli*
8/26/2010	Bridge Creek – approx. 75 m downstream of picnic area.	>2419 MPN/100 ml	140 /100 ml	220 MPN/100 ml

MPN= most probable number

Literature Cited

Barbour, M. T., J. Gerritsen, B. D. Snyder, and J. B. Stribling. 1999. Rapid Bioassessment Protocols for Use in Streams and Wadeable Rivers: Periphyton, Benthic Macroinvertebrates and Fish, Second Edition. EPA 841-B-99-002. U.S. Environmental Protection Agency.

Bell, J. and D. Hinson. 2010. Natural resource condition assessment: John Day Fossil Beds National Monument. Natural Resource Report NPS/UCBN/NRR—2010/174. National Park Service, Fort Collins, CO.

Garrett, L. K., T. J. Rodhouse, G. H. Dicus, C. C. Caudill, and M. R. Shardlow. 2007. Vitals Signs Monitoring Plan, Upper Columbia Basin Network. Natural Resource Report NPS/PWR/UCBN/NRR—2007/002. National Park Service, Fort Collins, CO.

Hall, J., Pollock, M., Hoh, S., 2010. Bridge Creek riparian restoration project 2010 planting plan. Draft V2.0. March 18, 2010. (http://www.nwfsc.noaa.gov/research/divisions/cbd/mathbio/isemp/docs/isemp_bridge_creek_2010plantingplan_20100526.pdf). Accessed 04 February 2011.

Heitke, J. D., E. J. Archer, D. D. Dugaw, B. A. Bouwes, E. A. Archer, R. C. Henderson, J. L. Kershner. 2008. Effectiveness monitoring for streams and riparian areas: sampling protocol for stream channel attributes. PACFISH/INFISH- Biological Opinion Effectiveness Monitoroing Program (PIBO-EM). Logan, UT. (http://www.fs.fed.us/biology/fishecology/emp). Accessed 18 January 2010.

Hilsenhoff, W. L. 1987. An improved biotic index of organic stream pollution. Great Lakes Entomologist **20**:31-39.

Hilsenhoff, W. L. 1988. Rapid field assessment of organic pollution with a family-level biotic index. Journal of the North American Benthological Society, **7**:65–68.

Irwin, R. J. 2008. Draft Part B lite QA/QC review checklist for aquatic vital sign monitoring protocols and SOPs, National Park Service, Water Resources Division. Fort Collins, CO. (http://www.nature.nps.gov/water/Vital_Signs_Guidance/Guidance_Documents/PartBLite.pdf). Accessed 18 February 2010.

ISEMP, 2009. ISEMP sampling protocol for stream channel attributes: Bridge Creek intensively monitored watershed. (http://www.nwfsc.noaa.gov/research/divisions/cbd/mathbio/isemp/docs/isemp_bridgehabitatsampling2009v1.pdf) Accessed 04 February 2011.

McCullough, D. A. 1999. A review and synthesis of effects of alterations to the water temperature regime on freshwater life stages of salmonids, with special reference to chinook salmon. EPA 910-R-99-010. U.S. Environmental Protection Agency, Washington, DC.

National Park Service (NPS) 1997. Baseline water quality data inventory and analysis: John Day Fossil Beds National Monument. NPS/NRWRD/NRTR-97/112. Fort Collins, CO.

National Park Service (NPS). 1999. Natural resource challenge: the National Park Service's action plan for preserving natural resources. US Department of the Interior National Park Service, Washington D.C. (http://www.nature.nps.gov/challenge/challengedoc/index.htm). Accessed 18 February 2010.

National Park Service (NPS). 2000. Strategic plan FY 2001-2005. NPS D-1383. US Department of the Interior National Park Service, Washington D.C. (http://planning.nps.gov/document/NPS_strategic_plan.pdf). Accessed 3 March 2011.

Olden, J. D., J. W. Adams, E. R. Larson. 2009. First record of Orconectes rusticus west of the great continental divide in North America. Crustaceana **82:** 1347-1351.

Oregon Department of Environmental Quality (OR DEQ). 2010. John Day River basin total maximum daily load (TMDL) and water quality management plan (WQMP). DEQ 10-WQ-025. Oregon Department of Environmental Quality. Portland, OR.

Pollock, M. 2007. Intensively monitored watershed restoration project Bridge Creek workplan-draft. Northwest Fisheries Science Center, NOAA-Fisheries. (http://www.nwfsc.noaa.gov/research/divisions/cbd/mathbio/isemp/docs/bc_proposal5_1_1_07.pdf). Accessed on 04 February 2011.

Starkey, E. N. 2011. Upper Columbia Basin Network stream channel characteristics and riparian condition annual report 2010: John Day Fossil Beds National Monument (JODA). Natural Resource Data Series NPS/UCBN/NRDS—2011/181. National Park Service, Fort Collins, CO. https://irma.nps.gov/App/Reference/DownloadDigitalFile?code=432851&file=UCBN_2010_StreamChannel_Riparian_Annual-Report_JODA_20110804_nrss.pdf Accessed 16 February 2012.

Starkey, E. N., L. K. Garrett, T. J. Rodhouse, G. H. Dicus, and R. K. Steinhorst. 2008. Upper Columbia Basin Network integrated water quality monitoring protocol: Narrative version 1.0. Natural Resource Report NPS/UCBN/NRR—2008/026. National Park Service, Fort Collins, CO. (http://science.nature.nps.gov/im/units/ucbn/reports/index.cfm#IWQ_Mon). Accessed 18 February 2010.

United States EPA. 2001. Environmental Monitoring and Assessment Program (EMAP): National Coastal Assessment Quality Assurance Project Plan 2001-2004. United States Environmental Protection Agency, Office of Research and Development, National Health and Environmental Effects Research Laboratory, Gulf Ecology Division, Gulf Breeze, FL.EPA/620/R-01/002.

United States EPA. 1995. Environmental Monitoring and Assessment Program (EMAP): Laboratory Methods Manual-Estuaries, Volume 1: Biological and Physical Analyses. U.S. Environmental Protection Agency, Office of Research and Development , Narragansett, RI. EPA/620/R-95/008.

Vannote, R. L., and B. W. Sweeney. 1980. Geographic analysis of thermal equilibria: a conceptual model for evaluating the effect of natural and modified thermal regimes on aquatic insect communities. The American Naturalist **115:** 667–695.

Wagner, R. J., R. W. Boulger Jr., C. J. Oblinger, and B. A. Smith. 2006. Guidelines and Standard procedures for continuous water-quality monitors: station operation, record computation, and data reporting: U.S. Geological Survey Techniques and Methods 1–D3, 51.

Weber, N. 2009. ISEMP field sampling and laboratory processing protocol for stream macroinvertebrates: Bridge Creek Intensively Monitored Watershed 2007 & 2008. EcoLogical, Inc. (http://www.nwfsc.noaa.gov/research/divisions/cbd/mathbio/isemp/docs/isemp_invert_protocol_2008_final_20090413.pdf) Accessed 04 February 2011.

Appendix A. 2010 Water Quality Monitoring Locations

Appendix A. 2010 Water Quality Monitoring Locations (continued)

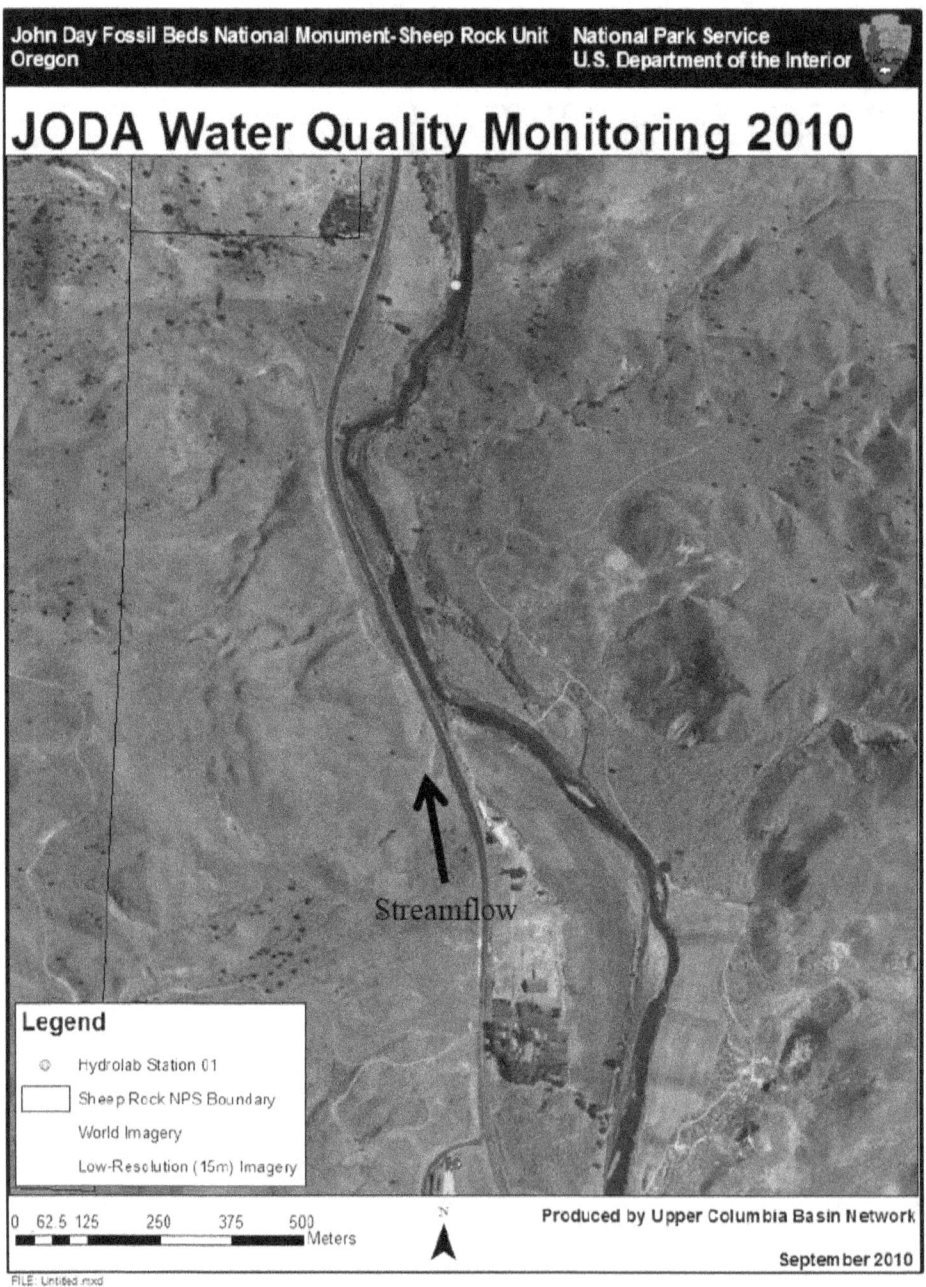

Appendix B. JODA Hydrologic Unit Code Boundaries

Appendix B. JODA Hydrologic Unit Code Boundaries (continued)

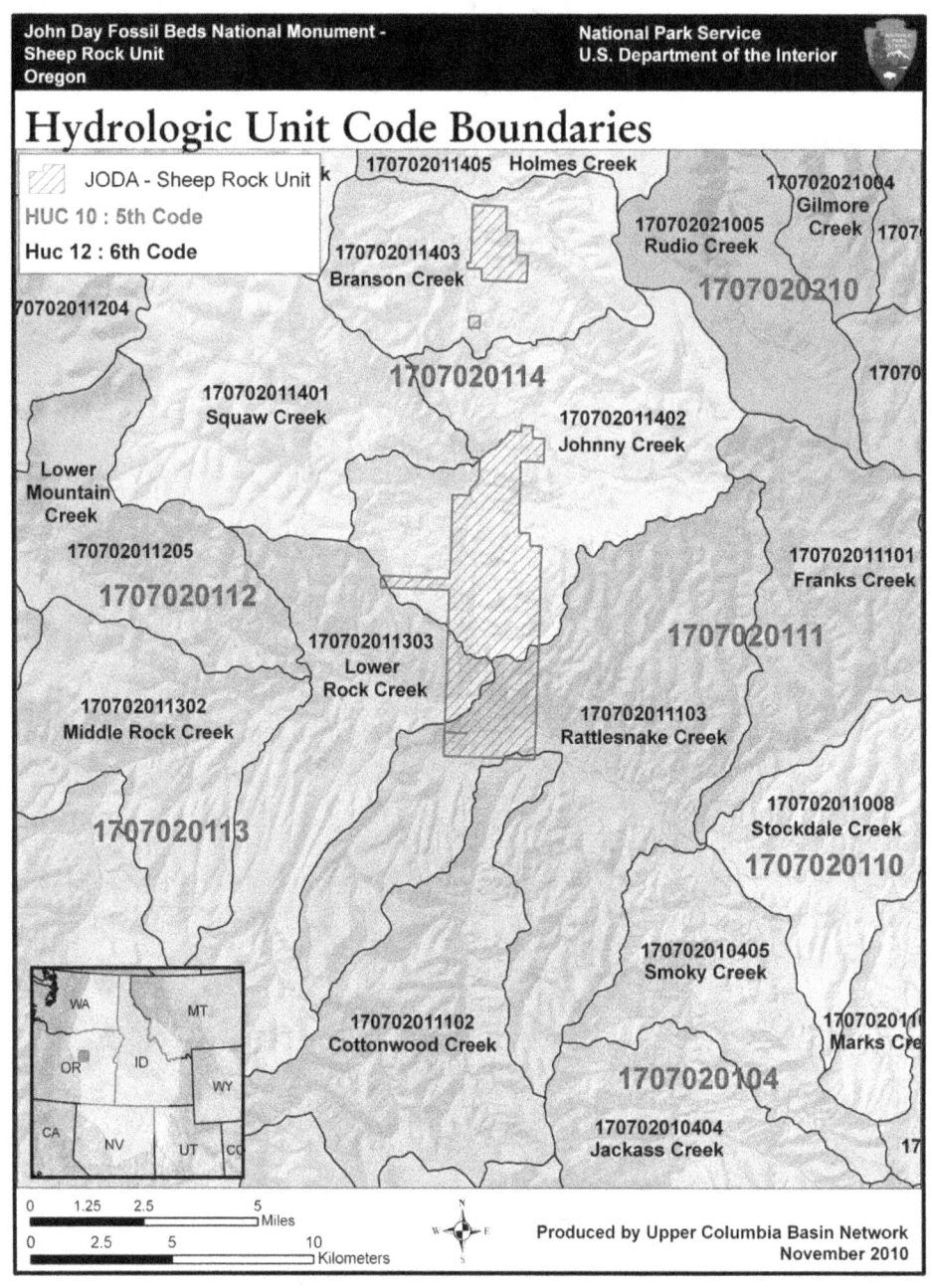

John Day Fossil Beds National Monument - Sheep Rock Unit
Oregon

National Park Service
U.S. Department of the Interior

Hydrologic Unit Code Boundaries

JODA - Sheep Rock Unit
HUC 10 : 5th Code
Huc 12 : 6th Code

170702011405 Holmes Creek

170702021004
Gilmore Creek

170702021005
Rudio Creek

1707020210

170702011403
Branson Creek

170702011204

1707020114

17070

170702011401
Squaw Creek

170702011402
Johnny Creek

Lower Mountain Creek

170702011205

1707020112

170702011101
Franks Creek

170702011303
Lower Rock Creek

1707020111

170702011302
Middle Rock Creek

170702011103
Rattlesnake Creek

1707020113

170702011008
Stockdale Creek

1707020110

170702010405
Smoky Creek

170702011102
Cottonwood Creek

1707020110
Marks Cre

1707020104

170702010404
Jackass Creek

17

WA
MT
OR
ID
WY
CA
NV
UT
CO

0 1.25 2.5 5 Miles
0 2.5 5 10 Kilometers

Produced by Upper Columbia Basin Network
November 2010

48

Appendix C. Sample Locations for Water Quality Monitoring at JODA

Park	Stream	Monitoring Type	Station #	Lat.	Long.	Y	X
JODA	Bridge Creek	Water Chemistry	001	44.65517177	-120.25189075	4949790.18	242167.86
JODA	John Day River	Water Chemistry	001	44.56650180	-119.64642028	4938202.31	289854.67
JODA	John Day River	Macroinvertebrate	3073	44.57885	-119.645	4939571	290011
JODA	John Day River	Macroinvertebrate	3074	44.5747	-119.646	4939113	289917
JODA	John Day River	Macroinvertebrate	3075	44.5672	-119.646	4938279	289889
JODA	John Day River	Macroinvertebrate	3076	44.56167	-119.647	4937668	289790
JODA	John Day River	Macroinvertebrate	3077	44.5575	-119.642	4937192	290172
JODA	John Day River	Macroinvertebrate	3078	44.55081	-119.642	4936449	290148

Note that X and Y have been projected in WGS84, UTM Zone 10 (Bridge Creek) Zone 11 (John Day River). These locations were recorded by the field crew with a handheld GPS unit.

49

Appendix D. Quality Control (QC) Indicators

QC data quality indicators for 2010 season at JODA- Sheep Rock, John Day River, Hydrolab #064, Station ID: JODA-Sheep Rock #001.

STORET Name	Units	Detection Range Description from Manufacture	Method Detection Limit (MDL)	Minimum Level of Quantitation (ML)	Alternative Measurement Sensitivity Plus (AMS+) Beginning of Season	Alternative Measurement Sensitivity Plus (AMS+) End of Season	Precision+ (RPD) Beginning of Season	Precision+ (RPD) End of Season
Temperature, water	deg C	-5 to 50°C	N/A	N/A	0.05	0.11	0.05	0.11
Specific Conductance	µS/cm	0 to 100,000 µS/cm	N/A	N/A	1.5	0.9	0.35	0.15
Dissolved Oxygen	mg/L	0-20 mg/L	N/A	N/A	0.05	0.07	0.10	0.10
pH	pH units	0-14 Units	N/A	N/A	0.06	0.05	0.12	0.00
Turbidity	NTU	0-3000 NTU	0.2	0.78	N/A	N/A	0.00	7.59

QC data quality indicators for 2010 season at JODA-Painted Hills, Bridge Creek Hydrolab #054, Station ID: JODA-Painted Hills #001.

STORET Name	Units	Detection Range Description from Manufacture	Method Detection Limit (MDL)	Minimum Level of Quantitation (ML)	Alternative Measurement Sensitivity Plus (AMS+) Beginning of Season	Alternative Measurement Sensitivity Plus (AMS+) End of Season	Precision+ (RPD) Beginning of Season	Precision+ (RPD) End of Season
Temperature, water	deg C	-5 to 50°C	N/A	N/A	0.04	0.06	0.07	0.00
Specific Conductance	µS/cm	0 to 100,000 µS/cm	N/A	N/A	0.6	1.1	0.03	0.06
Dissolved Oxygen	mg/L	0-20 mg/L	N/A	N/A	0.03	0.05	0.11	0.18
pH	pH units	0-14 Units	N/A	N/A	0.04	0.20	0.00	0.25
Turbidity	NTU	0-3000 NTU	0.3	0.81	N/A	N/A	0.00	2.02

51

Appendix E. Corrections History

Correction history for John Day River, JODA 2010 temperature data.			
Correction #	From	To	Comment
		No Corrections Applied	

Correction history for John Day River, JODA 2010 specific conductance data.			
Correction #	From	To	Comment
1	7/21/2010 20:00	7/21/2010 20:00	Delete Region due to outlier
2	8/1/2010 18:00	8/1/2010 18:00	Delete Region due to outlier
3	7/31/2010 21:00	7/31/2010 21:00	Delete Region due to outlier
4	7/31/2010 6:00	7/31/2010 6:00	Delete Region due to outlier
5	8/1/2010 7:00	8/1/2010 7:00	Delete Region due to outlier
6	6/25/2010 14:00	8/4/2010 6:00	
7	8/6/2010 11:00	8/6/2010 11:00	Delete Region due to outlier
8	8/13/2010 11:00	8/13/2010 11:00	Delete Region due to outlier
9	8/13/2010 20:00	8/13/2010 20:00	Delete Region due to outlier
10	8/14/2010 14:00	8/14/2010 14:00	Delete Region due to outlier
11	8/16/2010 11:00	8/16/2010 11:00	Delete Region due to outlier
12	8/17/2010 5:00	8/17/2010 5:00	Delete Region due to outlier
13	8/17/2010 7:00	8/17/2010 7:00	Delete Region due to outlier
14	8/17/2010 13:00	8/17/2010 13:00	Delete Region due to outlier
15	8/18/2010 11:00	8/18/2010 11:00	Delete Region due to outlier
16	8/19/2010 5:00	8/19/2010 5:00	Delete Region due to outlier
17	8/21/2010 8:00	8/21/2010 8:00	Delete Region due to outlier
18	8/25/2010 5:00	8/25/2010 5:00	Delete Region due to outlier
19	9/11/2010 11:00	9/11/2010 11:00	Delete Region due to outlier
20	9/12/2010 20:00	9/12/2010 20:00	Delete Region due to outlier
21	9/13/2010 2:00	9/13/2010 2:00	Delete Region due to outlier
22	9/14/2010 19:00	9/14/2010 20:00	Delete Region due to outlier
23	9/15/2010 5:00	9/15/2010 5:00	Delete Region due to outlier
24	9/15/2010 19:00	9/15/2010 19:00	Delete Region due to outlier
25	9/16/2010 6:00	9/16/2010 6:00	Delete Region due to outlier
26	9/16/2010 14:00	9/16/2010 14:00	Delete Region due to outlier
27	9/16/2010 19:00	9/16/2010 19:00	Delete Region due to outlier
28	9/17/2010 0:00	9/17/2010 0:00	Delete Region due to outlier
29	9/17/2010 3:00	9/17/2010 3:00	Delete Region due to outlier
30	9/17/2010 13:00	9/17/2010 13:00	Delete Region due to outlier
31	9/17/2010 17:00	9/17/2010 17:00	Delete Region due to outlier
32	9/18/2010 2:00	9/18/2010 2:00	Delete Region due to outlier

Appendix E. Corrections History (continued)

	Correction history for John Day River, JODA 2010 specific conductance data. (continued)		
Correction #	From	To	Comment
33	9/18/2010 14:00	9/18/2010 15:00	Delete Region due to outlier
34	9/19/2010 20:00	9/19/2010 20:00	Delete Region due to outlier
35	9/19/2010 23:00	9/19/2010 23:00	Delete Region due to outlier
36	9/30/2010 8:51	9/30/2010 10:27	Delete Region due to outlier
37	9/30/2010 11:51	9/30/2010 12:19	Delete Region due to outlier
38	9/30/2010 13:53	9/30/2010 14:09	Delete Region due to outlier
39	9/30/2010 15:38	9/30/2010 16:11	Delete Region due to outlier
40	10/4/2010 2:25	10/4/2010 3:29	Delete Region due to outlier
41	10/15/2010 3:43	10/15/2010 4:23	Delete Region due to outlier
42	10/15/2010 6:53	10/15/2010 8:20	Delete Region due to outlier
43	10/15/2010 9:24	10/15/2010 10:17	Delete Region due to outlier
44	10/15/2010 18:26	10/15/2010 19:29	Delete Region due to outlier
45	10/16/2010 3:33	10/16/2010 4:34	Delete Region due to outlier
46	10/16/2010 6:28	10/16/2010 7:40	Delete Region due to outlier
47	10/16/2010 13:41	10/16/2010 14:27	Delete Region due to outlier
48	10/16/2010 20:31	10/16/2010 21:24	Delete Region due to outlier
49	10/17/2010 7:35	10/17/2010 8:26	Delete Region due to outlier
50	10/18/2010 5:43	10/18/2010 6:37	Delete Region due to outlier
51	10/19/2010 13:32	10/19/2010 14:56	Delete Region due to outlier
52	10/20/2010 19:44	10/20/2010 20:22	Delete Region due to outlier
53	10/21/2010 6:48	10/21/2010 8:55	Delete Region due to outlier
54	10/22/2010 17:45	10/22/2010 18:18	Delete Region due to outlier
55	10/24/2010 15:43	10/24/2010 16:29	Delete Region due to outlier
56	10/24/2010 17:53	10/24/2010 18:21	Delete Region due to outlier
57	10/24/2010 21:29	10/24/2010 22:43	Delete Region due to outlier
58	10/26/2010 18:32	10/26/2010 19:23	Delete Region due to outlier
59	10/27/2010 7:43	10/27/2010 8:16	Delete Region due to outlier
60	10/27/2010 23:35	10/28/2010 1:32	Delete Region due to outlier
61	10/28/2010 16:56	10/28/2010 17:21	Delete Region due to outlier
62	10/29/2010 5:52	10/29/2010 6:15	Delete Region due to outlier
63	10/29/2010 7:49	10/29/2010 11:08	Delete Region due to outlier
64	10/30/2010 2:49	10/30/2010 5:22	Delete Region due to outlier
65	10/16/2010 22:11	10/17/2010 1:26	Delete Region due to outlier
66	10/15/2010 10:11	10/15/2010 16:15	Delete Region due to outlier
67	10/17/2010 4:28	10/17/2010 6:31	Delete Region due to outlier
68	10/17/2010 18:33	10/17/2010 20:24	Delete Region due to outlier

Appendix E. Corrections History (continued)

Correction history for John Day River, JODA 2010 specific conductance data. (continued)			
Correction #	From	To	Comment
69	10/18/2010 23:36	10/19/2010 0:35	Delete Region due to outlier
70	10/19/2010 20:51	10/19/2010 21:24	Delete Region due to outlier
71	10/20/2010 4:33	10/20/2010 6:43	Delete Region due to outlier
72	10/21/2010 3:32	10/21/2010 4:57	Delete Region due to outlier
73	10/22/2010 14:20	10/22/2010 15:51	Delete Region due to outlier
74	10/22/2010 20:37	10/23/2010 1:36	Delete Region due to outlier
75	10/23/2010 3:07	10/23/2010 4:45	Delete Region due to outlier
76	10/23/2010 5:30	10/23/2010 7:27	Delete Region due to outlier
77	10/23/2010 21:20	10/24/2010 0:35	Delete Region due to outlier
78	10/24/2010 2:32	10/24/2010 5:41	Delete Region due to outlier
79	10/24/2010 6:39	10/24/2010 7:31	Delete Region due to outlier
80	10/24/2010 12:18	10/24/2010 14:47	Delete Region due to outlier
81	10/26/2010 0:17	10/26/2010 1:42	Delete Region due to outlier
82	10/26/2010 2:21	10/26/2010 5:55	Delete Region due to outlier
83	10/26/2010 11:27	10/26/2010 12:45	Delete Region due to outlier
84	10/27/2010 2:18	10/27/2010 6:51	Delete Region due to outlier
85	10/28/2010 11:15	10/28/2010 13:38	Delete Region due to outlier
86	10/29/2010 14:34	10/29/2010 15:26	Delete Region due to outlier
87	10/30/2010 7:16	10/30/2010 8:47	Delete Region due to outlier
88	10/30/2010 11:36	10/30/2010 12:15	Delete Region due to outlier
89	10/30/2010 13:27	10/30/2010 14:58	Delete Region due to outlier
90	10/30/2010 17:34	10/30/2010 18:19	Delete Region due to outlier
91	10/31/2010 3:19	10/31/2010 4:57	Delete Region due to outlier
92	10/31/2010 6:54	10/31/2010 7:07	Delete Region due to outlier
93	10/31/2010 12:32	10/31/2010 15:47	Delete Region due to outlier
94	10/31/2010 22:35	10/31/2010 23:49	Delete Region due to outlier
95	11/1/2010 2:16	11/1/2010 4:39	Delete Region due to outlier
96	11/1/2010 6:19	11/1/2010 8:09	Delete Region due to outlier
97	11/1/2010 9:26	11/1/2010 10:21	Delete Region due to outlier
98	11/1/2010 14:23	11/1/2010 15:51	Delete Region due to outlier
99	11/1/2010 17:38	11/1/2010 19:20	Delete Region due to outlier
100	11/2/2010 11:40	11/2/2010 13:14	Delete Region due to outlier
101	11/2/2010 14:38	11/2/2010 15:13	Delete Region due to outlier
102	11/2/2010 23:18	11/3/2010 0:23	Delete Region due to outlier
103	11/3/2010 7:34	11/3/2010 8:21	Delete Region due to outlier
104	11/3/2010 16:46	11/3/2010 17:25	Delete Region due to outlier

Appendix E. Corrections History (continued)

Correction history for John Day River, JODA 2010 specific conductance data. (continued)

Correction #	From	To	Comment
105	11/4/2010 0:46	11/4/2010 3:15	Delete Region due to outlier
106	11/4/2010 5:41	11/4/2010 6:23	Delete Region due to outlier
107	9/29/2010 13:00	11/5/2010 2:01	Drift Correction with Calibration Drift value of 0.550 and Fouling Drift value of 5.800

Correction history for John Day River, JODA 2010 dissolved oxygen data.

Correction #	From	To	Comment
1	8/4/2010 15:00	8/25/2010 10:00	Drift Correction with Calibration Drift value of 0.120 and Fouling Drift value of -0.810

Correction history for John Day River, JODA 2010 pH data.

Correction #	From	To	Comment
1	6/25/2010 14:00	8/4/2010 6:00	Drift Correction with Calibration Drift value of -0.130 and Fouling Drift value of 0.080

Correction history for John Day River, JODA 2010 turbidity data.

Correction #	From	To	Comment
1	7/3/2010 13:00	7/3/2010 13:00	Delete Region due to outlier
2	7/11/2010 6:00	7/11/2010 6:00	Delete Region due to outlier
3	7/17/2010 19:00	7/17/2010 19:00	Delete Region due to outlier
4	7/23/2010 1:00	7/23/2010 1:00	Delete Region due to outlier
5	7/25/2010 12:00	7/25/2010 12:00	Delete Region due to outlier
6	7/27/2010 7:00	7/27/2010 7:00	Delete Region due to outlier
7	7/26/2010 17:00	7/26/2010 17:00	Delete Region due to outlier
8	7/28/2010 13:00	7/28/2010 13:00	Delete Region due to outlier
9	7/31/2010 17:00	7/31/2010 17:00	Delete Region due to outlier
10	7/1/2010 15:00	7/1/2010 15:00	Delete Region due to outlier
11	7/2/2010 8:00	7/2/2010 8:00	Delete Region due to outlier
12	7/2/2010 16:00	7/2/2010 16:00	Delete Region due to outlier
13	7/5/2010 9:00	7/5/2010 9:00	Delete Region due to outlier
14	7/13/2010 19:00	7/13/2010 19:00	Delete Region due to outlier
15	7/17/2010 11:00	7/17/2010 11:00	Delete Region due to outlier
16	7/17/2010 15:00	7/17/2010 15:00	Delete Region due to outlier
17	7/18/2010 20:00	7/18/2010 20:00	Delete Region due to outlier
18	7/20/2010 1:00	7/20/2010 1:00	Delete Region due to outlier
19	7/22/2010 19:00	7/22/2010 19:00	Delete Region due to outlier
20	7/25/2010 19:00	7/25/2010 19:00	Delete Region due to outlier
21	7/28/2010 21:00	7/28/2010 21:00	Delete Region due to outlier

Appendix E. Corrections History (continued)

	Correction history for John Day River, JODA 2010 turbidity data. (continued)		
Correction #	From	To	Comment
22	7/29/2010 15:00	7/29/2010 15:00	Delete Region due to outlier
23	7/29/2010 19:00	7/29/2010 19:00	Delete Region due to outlier
24	7/31/2010 9:00	7/31/2010 9:00	Delete Region due to outlier
25	6/26/2010 12:00	6/26/2010 12:00	Delete Region due to outlier
26	6/27/2010 4:00	6/27/2010 4:00	Delete Region due to outlier
27	6/24/2010 21:03	8/5/2010 4:35	Drift Correction with Calibration Drift value of -2.450 and Fouling Drift value of -1.100
28	6/25/2010 14:00	8/4/2010 6:00	
29	8/6/2010 20:00	8/6/2010 20:00	Delete Region due to outlier
30	8/8/2010 0:00	8/8/2010 0:00	Delete Region due to outlier
31	8/8/2010 8:00	8/8/2010 8:00	Delete Region due to outlier
32	8/8/2010 15:00	8/8/2010 15:00	Delete Region due to outlier
33	8/10/2010 5:00	8/10/2010 5:00	Delete Region due to outlier
34	8/11/2010 13:00	8/11/2010 13:00	Delete Region due to outlier
35	9/5/2010 23:00	9/5/2010 23:00	Delete Region due to outlier
36	9/8/2010 7:00	9/8/2010 7:00	Delete Region due to outlier
37	9/8/2010 9:00	9/8/2010 9:00	Delete Region due to outlier
38	9/11/2010 8:00	9/11/2010 8:00	Delete Region due to outlier
39	9/13/2010 7:00	9/13/2010 7:00	Delete Region due to outlier
40	9/15/2010 7:00	9/15/2010 7:00	Delete Region due to outlier
41	9/15/2010 11:00	9/15/2010 11:00	Delete Region due to outlier
42	9/15/2010 16:00	9/15/2010 16:00	Delete Region due to outlier
43	9/16/2010 7:00	9/16/2010 8:00	Delete Region due to outlier
44	9/8/2010 19:00	9/8/2010 19:00	Delete point(s)
45	9/8/2010 22:00	9/8/2010 22:00	Delete point(s)
46	9/30/2010 8:00	9/30/2010 8:00	Delete Region due to outlier
47	9/30/2010 11:00	9/30/2010 11:00	Delete Region due to outlier
48	9/30/2010 12:00	9/30/2010 12:00	Delete Region due to outlier
49	10/1/2010 9:00	10/1/2010 9:00	Delete Region due to outlier
50	10/1/2010 11:00	10/1/2010 11:00	Delete Region due to outlier
51	10/1/2010 16:00	10/1/2010 18:00	Delete Region due to outlier
52	10/2/2010 5:00	10/2/2010 5:00	Delete Region due to outlier
53	10/2/2010 7:00	10/2/2010 7:00	Delete Region due to outlier
54	10/2/2010 9:00	10/2/2010 9:00	Delete Region due to outlier
55	10/2/2010 11:00	10/2/2010 14:00	Delete Region due to outlier
56	10/2/2010 18:00	10/2/2010 18:00	Delete Region due to outlier
57	10/3/2010 9:00	10/3/2010 9:00	Delete Region due to outlier

Appendix E. Corrections History (continued)

	Correction history for John Day River, JODA 2010 turbidity data. (continued)		
Correction #	From	To	Comment
58	10/3/2010 11:00	10/3/2010 11:00	Delete Region due to outlier
59	10/4/2010 7:00	10/4/2010 19:00	Delete Region due to outlier
60	10/5/2010 3:00	10/5/2010 3:00	Delete Region due to outlier
61	10/5/2010 7:00	10/5/2010 7:00	Delete Region due to outlier
62	10/5/2010 16:00	10/5/2010 16:00	Delete Region due to outlier
63	10/7/2010 2:00	10/7/2010 2:00	Delete Region due to outlier
64	10/10/2010 3:00	10/10/2010 3:00	Delete Region due to outlier
65	10/11/2010 17:00	10/11/2010 17:00	Delete Region due to outlier
66	10/14/2010 14:00	10/14/2010 14:00	Delete Region due to outlier
67	10/14/2010 19:00	10/14/2010 19:00	Delete Region due to outlier
68	10/15/2010 7:00	10/15/2010 7:00	Delete Region due to outlier
69	10/16/2010 4:00	10/16/2010 4:00	Delete Region due to outlier
70	10/16/2010 15:00	10/16/2010 15:00	Delete Region due to outlier
71	10/16/2010 17:00	10/16/2010 17:00	Delete Region due to outlier
72	10/16/2010 21:00	10/16/2010 21:00	Delete Region due to outlier
73	10/18/2010 15:00	10/18/2010 16:00	Delete Region due to outlier
74	10/19/2010 8:52	11/4/2010 23:28	Delete Region due to outlier

Appendix E. Corrections History (continued)

Correction history for Bridge Creek, JODA 2010 temperature data.

Correction #	From	To	Comment
		No Corrections Applied	

Correction history for Bridge Creek, JODA 2010 specific conductance data.

Correction #	From	To	Comment
1	6/26/2010 11:00	8/5/2010 5:00	Drift Correction with Calibration Drift value of 1.650 and Fouling Drift value of 5.400
2	8/25/2010 9:00	9/29/2010 13:00	Drift Correction with Calibration Drift value of -0.450 and Fouling Drift value of -19.700
3	10/12/2010 12:36	10/12/2010 14:21	Delete Region due to outlier
4	10/16/2010 2:03	10/16/2010 3:35	Delete Region due to outlier
5	9/29/2010 18:00	11/4/2010 15:03	Drift Correction with Calibration Drift value of 8.250 and Fouling Drift value of 1.200

Correction history for Bridge Creek, JODA 2010 dissolved oxygen data.

Correction #	From	To	Comment
1	9/29/2010 18:00	11/3/2010 8:00	Drift Correction with Calibration Drift value of 0.520 and Fouling Drift value of 0.170

Correction history for Bridge Creek, JODA 2010 pH data.

Correction #	From	To	Comment
1	6/26/2010 11:00	8/5/2010 5:00	Drift Correction with Calibration Drift value of -0.550 and Fouling Drift value of 0.030
2	10/20/2010 15:00	10/20/2010 15:00	Delete Region due to outlier

Correction history for Bridge Creek, JODA 2010 turbidity data.

Correction #	From	To	Comment
1	7/17/2010 6:00	7/17/2010 6:00	Delete Region due to outlier
2	7/21/2010 15:00	7/21/2010 15:00	Delete Region due to outlier
3	6/26/2010 2:20	8/5/2010 20:03	Drift Correction with Calibration Drift value of -5.500 and Fouling Drift value of 11.500
4	6/26/2010 11:00	8/5/2010 5:00	
5	9/15/2010 10:00	9/15/2010 10:00	Delete Region due to outlier
6	9/19/2010 14:00	9/19/2010 14:00	Delete Region due to outlier
7	8/25/2010 9:00	9/30/2010 14:24	Drift Correction with Calibration Drift value of -0.150 and Fouling Drift value of 2.800
8	10/3/2010 7:00	10/3/2010 7:00	Delete Region due to outlier
9	10/5/2010 18:00	10/5/2010 18:00	Delete Region due to outlier
10	10/15/2010 7:00	10/15/2010 7:00	Delete Region due to outlier
11	10/15/2010 14:00	10/15/2010 14:00	Delete Region due to outlier

Appendix E. Corrections History (continued)

	Correction history for Bridge Creek, JODA 2010 turbidity data. (continued)		
Correction #	From	To	Comment
12	10/16/2010 2:00	10/16/2010 2:00	Delete Region due to outlier
13	10/16/2010 7:00	10/16/2010 7:00	Delete Region due to outlier
14	10/18/2010 7:00	10/18/2010 7:00	Delete Region due to outlier
15	10/19/2010 7:00	10/19/2010 7:00	Delete Region due to outlier
16	9/29/2010 18:00	11/4/2010 12:12	Drift Correction with Calibration Drift value of -1.900 and Fouling Drift value of 0.300

Appendix F. Macroinvertebrate Metrics

NPS Upper Columbia Basin Benthos 2010 – JODA
*Standardized to OTU and fixed count

SampleID	146650	146651	146652	146653	146654	146655
Station (NAMC)	PIBO:3073	PIBO:3074	PIBO:3075	PIBO:3076	PIBO:3077	PIBO:3078
Station (Customer)	5871	5872	5873	5874	5875	5876
Waterbody	John Day	John Day	John Day	John Day	John Day	John Day
County	Grant	Grant	Grant	Grant	Grant	Grant
State	OR	OR	OR	OR	OR	OR
Latitude	44.578845	44.574695	44.567196	44.561671	44.557497	44.550814
Longitude	-119.644871	-119.646357	-119.646216	-119.647281	-119.641573	-119.641803
Collection Date	8/17/2010	8/18/2010	8/19/2010	8/20/2010	8/20/2010	8/20/2010
Habitat Sampled	Targeted Riffle	Targeted Riffle	Targeted Riffle	Targeted Riffle	Targeted Riffle	Targeted Riffle
Collection Method	Surber Net	Surber Net	Surber Net	Surber Net	Surber Net	Surber Net
Field Notes	NULL	NULL	NULL	NULL	NULL	NULL
Lab Notes	NULL	NULL	NULL	NULL	NULL	NULL
Area sampled (m^2)	0.74	0.74	0.74	0.74	0.74	0.74
Field Split	100	100	100	100	100	100
Lab Split	18.75	100	37.5	75	12.5	25
Split Count	703	801	643	755	579	683
Fixed Count	300	300	300	300	300	300
Big Rare Count	23	0	29	18	33	43
Richness*	22	31	29	22	23	28
Abundance	5098	1082	2356	1385	6304	3750
Shannon's Diversity*	2.44784389	2.931645135	2.834427637	2.47456294	1.881243328	2.716594574
Simpson's Diversity*	0.888896321	0.929453735	0.927424749	0.874604236	0.740423634	0.916700111
Evenness*	0.791915325	0.853714636	0.841751892	0.800559351	0.599983032	0.815254456
# of EPT Taxa*	11	19	18	13	15	18
EPT Taxa Abundance	3534	857	1863	836	2493	2515
Dominant Family	Heptageniidae	Heptageniidae	Heptageniidae	Baetidae	Simuliidae	Baetidae

Appendix F. Macroinvertebrate Metrics (continued)

NPS Upper Columbia Basin Benthos 2010 – JODA
*Standardized to OTU and fixed count

SampleID	146650	146651	146652	146653	146654	146655
Station (NAMC)	PIBO:3073	PIBO:3074	PIBO:3075	PIBO:3076	PIBO:3077	PIBO:3078
Station (Customer)	5871	5872	5873	5874	5875	5876
Waterbody	John Day	John Day	John Day	John Day	John Day	John Day
County	Grant	Grant	Grant	Grant	Grant	Grant
State	OR	OR	OR	OR	OR	OR
Latitude	44.578845	44.574695	44.567196	44.561671	44.557497	44.550814
Longitude	-119.644871	-119.646357	-119.646216	-119.647281	-119.641573	-119.641803
Collection Date	8/17/2010	8/18/2010	8/19/2010	8/20/2010	8/20/2010	8/20/2010
Habitat Sampled	Targeted Riffle	Targeted Riffle	Targeted Riffle	Targeted Riffle	Targeted Riffle	Targeted Riffle
Collection Method	Surber Net	Surber Net	Surber Net	Surber Net	Surber Net	Surber Net
Abundance of Dominant Family	1396	376	634	316	2600	1012
Dominant Taxa	Simulium	Heptageniidae	Heptageniidae	Orthocladiinae	Simulium	Baetis
Abundance of Dominant Taxa	859	222	371	254	2514	524
Hilsenhoff Biotic Index*	4.24	3.256666667	3.24	4.24	4.853333333	3.72
# of Intolerant Taxa*	1	5	6	4	5	6
Intolerant Taxa abundance	138	192	220	61	111	132
# of Tolerant Taxa*	0	0	0	0	1	0
Tolerant Taxa abundance	0	0	0	0	11	0
USFS Community Tolerance Quotient (d)*	79	72	68	78	77	71
# of shredder taxa*	1	1	1	1	0	1
Shredder Abundance	14	0	0	0	0	0
# of scraper taxa*	2	2	6	2	2	2
Scraper abundance	1033	272	527	263	216	542
# of collector-filterer taxa*	3	4	4	2	3	3
Collector-filterer abundance	1598	127	458	329	3673	1103
# of collector-gatherer taxa*	8	13	9	9	9	13

Appendix F. Macroinvertebrate Metrics (continued)

NPS Upper Columbia Basin Benthos 2010 – JODA
*Standardized to OTU and fixed count

SampleID	146650	146651	146652	146653	146654	146655
Station (NAMC)	PIBO:3073	PIBO:3074	PIBO:3075	PIBO:3076	PIBO:3077	PIBO:3078
Station (Customer)	5871	5872	5873	5874	5875	5876
Waterbody	John Day	John Day	John Day	John Day	John Day	John Day
County	Grant	Grant	Grant	Grant	Grant	Grant
State	OR	OR	OR	OR	OR	OR
Latitude	44.578845	44.574695	44.567196	44.561671	44.557497	44.550814
Longitude	-119.644871	-119.646357	-119.646216	-119.647281	-119.641573	-119.641803
Collection Date	8/17/2010	8/18/2010	8/19/2010	8/20/2010	8/20/2010	8/20/2010
Habitat Sampled	Targeted Riffle	Targeted Riffle	Targeted Riffle	Targeted Riffle	Targeted Riffle	Targeted Riffle
Collection Method	Surber Net	Surber Net	Surber Net	Surber Net	Surber Net	Surber Net
Collector-gatherer abundance	1832	566	1133	635	1895	1464
# of predator taxa*	2	4	5	4	5	4
Predator abundance	52	49	86	52	109	153
# of clinger taxa*	10	12	13	8	9	11
Long-lived Taxa*	5	5	5	4	5	6
# of Ephemeroptera taxa*	6	11	8	7	7	9
Ephemeroptera abundance	2318	696	1330	574	1224	1577
# of Plecoptera taxa*	1	2	3	3	3	3
Plecoptera abundance	16	19	64	39	66	66
# of Trichoptera taxa*	4	6	7	3	5	6
Trichoptera abundance	1200	142	469	223	1203	872
# of Coleoptera taxa*	4	4	3	3	2	4
Coleoptera abundance	323	50	186	105	249	630
# of Elmidae Taxa*	3	3	2	2	2	3
Elmidae abundance	166	23	95	81	249	591
# of Megaloptera taxa*	0	0	0	0	0	0

Appendix F. Macroinvertebrate Metrics (continued)

NPS Upper Columbia Basin Benthos 2010 – JODA
*Standardized to OTU and fixed count

SampleID	146650	146651	146652	146653	146654	146655
Station (NAMC)	PIBO:3073	PIBO:3074	PIBO:3075	PIBO:3076	PIBO:3077	PIBO:3078
Station (Customer)	5871	5872	5873	5874	5875	5876
Waterbody	John Day	John Day	John Day	John Day	John Day	John Day
County	Grant	Grant	Grant	Grant	Grant	Grant
State	OR	OR	OR	OR	OR	OR
Latitude	44.578845	44.574695	44.567196	44.561671	44.557497	44.550814
Longitude	-119.644871	-119.646357	-119.646216	-119.647281	-119.641573	-119.641803
Collection Date	8/17/2010	8/18/2010	8/19/2010	8/20/2010	8/20/2010	8/20/2010
Habitat Sampled	Targeted Riffle	Targeted Riffle	Targeted Riffle	Targeted Riffle	Targeted Riffle	Targeted Riffle
Collection Method	Surber Net	Surber Net	Surber Net	Surber Net	Surber Net	Surber Net
Megaloptera abundance	0	0	0	0	0	0
# of Diptera taxa*	4	4	4	4	4	3
Diptera abundance	1183	100	184	418	3541	524
# of Chironomidae taxa*	2	3	2	3	3	2
Chironomidae abundance	317	96	162	301	941	222
# of Crustacea taxa*	0	0	0	0	0	0
Crustacea abundance	0	0	0	0	0	0
# of Oligochaete taxa*	0	0	0	0	0	0
Oligochaete abundance	0	41	94	0	0	0
# of Mollusca taxa*	0	0	1	0	0	0
Mollusca abundance	0	0	4	0	0	0
# of Insect taxa*	20	28	26	21	23	27
Insect abundance	5062	1018	2250	1376	6304	3691
# of Non-insect taxa*	1	3	3	1	0	1
Non-insect abundance	36	65	106	9	0	59

Appendix G. Macroinvertebrate Taxa List

NPS Upper Columbia Basin Benthos 2011 – NEPE
Note that all samples were from targeted riffles and sampled using Surber nets.

SAMPLE	STATION	NAME	SAMP DATE	LAB SPLIT	AREA	TSN	CODE	TAXON	Split Count	Big Rare Count	DENSITY (#/m2)
147160	PIBO:3118	Jim Ford 4	8/19/2011	100	0.74	76484	927	Lymnaea	1		1
147160	PIBO:3118	Jim Ford 4	8/19/2011	100	0.74	127917	180	Chironomidae	1		1
147160	PIBO:3118	Jim Ford 4	8/19/2011	100	0.74	127994	187	Tanypodinae	1		1
147160	PIBO:3118	Jim Ford 4	8/19/2011	100	0.74	128457	184	Orthocladiinae	15		20
147160	PIBO:3118	Jim Ford 4	8/19/2011	100	0.74	93294	69	Amphipoda	3		4
147160	PIBO:3118	Jim Ford 4	8/19/2011	100	0.74	97336	82	Cambaridae	1		1
147160	PIBO:3118	Jim Ford 4	8/19/2011	100	0.74	129228	182	Chironominae	5		7
147159	PIBO:3116	Jim Ford 2	8/18/2011	100	0.74	102077	374	Coenagrionidae	1		1
147159	PIBO:3116	Jim Ford 2	8/18/2011	100	0.74	113166	683	Hydrochus	1		1
147159	PIBO:3116	Jim Ford 2	8/18/2011	100	0.74	128457	184	Orthocladiinae	17		23
147159	PIBO:3116	Jim Ford 2	8/18/2011	100	0.74	129228	182	Chironominae	6		8
147159	PIBO:3116	Jim Ford 2	8/18/2011	100	0.74	93294	69	Amphipoda	2		3
147159	PIBO:3116	Jim Ford 2	8/18/2011	100	0.74	100903	251	Callibaetis	1		1
147159	PIBO:3116	Jim Ford 2	8/18/2011	100	0.74	101478	261	Caenis	1		1
147159	PIBO:3116	Jim Ford 2	8/18/2011	100	0.74	127994	187	Tanypodinae	1		1
147157	PIBO:3114	Lapwai	8/20/2011	9.38	0.74	83005	66	Sperchonidae	16		231
147157	PIBO:3114	Lapwai	8/20/2011	9.38	0.74	114205	144	Zaitzevia	2		29
147157	PIBO:3114	Lapwai	8/20/2011	9.38	0.74	115398	495	Hydropsychidae	15		216
147157	PIBO:3114	Lapwai	8/20/2011	9.38	0.74	115408	497	Cheumatopsyche	36	1	520
147157	PIBO:3114	Lapwai	8/20/2011	9.38	0.74	115453	499	Hydropsyche	31	1	448
147157	PIBO:3114	Lapwai	8/20/2011	9.38	0.74	115629	506	Hydroptilidae	1		14
147157	PIBO:3114	Lapwai	8/20/2011	9.38	0.74	127994	187	Tanypodinae	4		58
147157	PIBO:3114	Lapwai	8/20/2011	9.38	0.74	135830	200	Empididae	1		14
147157	PIBO:3114	Lapwai	8/20/2011	9.38	0.74	82769	58	Trombidiformes	11		158
147157	PIBO:3114	Lapwai	8/20/2011	9.38	0.74	100626	280	Epeorus	3		43

Appendix G. Macroinvertebrate Taxa List (continued)

NPS Upper Columbia Basin Benthos 2011 – NEPE
Note that all samples were from targeted riffles and sampled using Surber nets.

SAMPLE	STATION	NAME	SAMPDATE	LAB SPLIT	AREA	TSN	CODE	TAXON	Split Count	Big Rare Count	DENSITY (#/m2)
147157	PIBO:3114	Lapwai	8/20/2011	9.38	0.74	100800	250	Baetis	25	2	363
147157	PIBO:3114	Lapwai	8/20/2011	9.38	0.74	103102	469	Skwala	0	1	1
147157	PIBO:3114	Lapwai	8/20/2011	9.38	0.74	114093	121	Elmidae	4	0	58
147157	PIBO:3114	Lapwai	8/20/2011	9.38	0.74	114177	135	Optioservus	2	0	29
147157	PIBO:3114	Lapwai	8/20/2011	9.38	0.74	114180	1076	Optioservus quadrimaculatus	1	0	14
147157	PIBO:3114	Lapwai	8/20/2011	9.38	0.74	115095	480	Trichoptera	4	0	58
147157	PIBO:3114	Lapwai	8/20/2011	9.38	0.74	116318	1488	Onocosmoecus unicolor	1	0	14
147157	PIBO:3114	Lapwai	8/20/2011	9.38	0.74	117159	491	Glossosoma	3	1	45
147157	PIBO:3114	Lapwai	8/20/2011	9.38	0.74	117682	350	Petrophila	1	0	14
147157	PIBO:3114	Lapwai	8/20/2011	9.38	0.74	126640	221	Simuliidae	113	0	1628
147157	PIBO:3114	Lapwai	8/20/2011	9.38	0.74	126774	223	Simulium	186	3	2684
147157	PIBO:3114	Lapwai	8/20/2011	9.38	0.74	127917	180	Chironomidae	27	0	389
147157	PIBO:3114	Lapwai	8/20/2011	9.38	0.74	128457	184	Orthocladiinae	177	3	2554
147157	PIBO:3114	Lapwai	8/20/2011	9.38	0.74	129228	182	Chironominae	61	0	879
147157	PIBO:3114	Lapwai	8/20/2011	9.38	0.74	563956	652	Nemata	1	0	14
147157	PIBO:3114	Lapwai	8/20/2011	9.38	0.74	568598	834	Diphetor hageni	6	0	86

The Department of the Interior protects and manages the nation's natural resources and cultural heritage; provides scientific and other information about those resources; and honors its special responsibilities to American Indians, Alaska Natives, and affiliated Island Communities.

NPS 177/114294, June 2012

www.ingramcontent.com/pod-product-compliance
Lightning Source LLC
Chambersburg PA
CBHW081137290526
45795CB00006B/2271